THIS IS CALIFORNIA:
PLEASE KEEP OUT!

Also by Art Seidenbaum

Confrontation on Campus

THIS IS CALIFORNIA: PLEASE KEEP OUT!

ART SEIDENBAUM

PETER H. WYDEN/PUBLISHER
New York

*To Lida, who brought me into New York life, and
To Patricia, who keeps me from it.*

THIS IS CALIFORNIA:
PLEASE KEEP OUT!

COPYRIGHT © 1975 BY Art Seidenbaum

All rights reserved, including the right to reproduce
this book, or parts thereof, in any form, except for the
inclusion of brief quotations in a review.

Library of Congress Cataloging in Publication Data

Seidenbaum, Art.
      This is California, please keep out!

      1. California—Social life and customs. I. Title.
F866.2.S43   917.94'03'5   74-14975
ISBN 0-88326-094-8

MANUFACTURED IN THE UNITED STATES OF AMERICA

Acknowledgements

Thanks to the Donner Party, for not stopping.
Thanks to all the other Americans who preferred to
stay home.

Contents

From Out of the West

The sexual revolution did not necessarily begin in the West, and senseless violence was not created in the East.

The first nude swimming party I ever attended happened in Bryn Mawr, Pennsylvania, on a summer night when a circle of academic people decided to crawl without their clothes.

The first time I was assaulted by a stranger—he simply stopped to beat me up without provocation—was in Portland, Oregon, on a drizzly winter night.

Not all American myths about geography are true.

But people *are* shaped by where they are, and people are characterized by where they choose to be. I choose to be in California, and I believe it is now necessary to put the East and its people in their place.

I remember the Brooklyn cab driver who took me

to Kennedy International and asked all kinds of questions about California. He was sick, he said. Sick of being ordered around by impatient businessmen. Sick of being ticketed by dumb policemen. Sick of pushers, prostitutes, and people in general. He was also sick of the gout. He wondered if the climate in California would be good for all that ailed him.

I said I liked living in Los Angeles, but I didn't think gout would go away with different weather.

"Well, it don't matter," he decided. "I got my plot paid for in Queens, and if I die in L.A. I don't know nobody who'd ship my body back."

That is an East Coast attitude.

I remember my single friend in Washington, D.C., who showed me her apartment in a handsome old renovated brick walkup. She had beautiful brass kitchen utensils. She had excellent modern prints. She had antique lamps and Oriental rugs. She also had a heavy rope hanging by her bedroom window, on the inside. While a would-be robber or rapist was working his way through the three locks on the front door, she would have time to run to the bedroom, throw the rope down along the outside wall, and lower herself into the alley.

That is an East Coast idea of security.

And I remember writer Richard Armstrong arriving in Los Angeles from his home in New York, gaping at the glare and blur and billboards of the West. He squinted several times and said, "None of my grandchildren will be Californians."

That is East Coast bigotry.

Most of what follows is West Coast bigotry.

-I-

American Refugees

California is where Americans have come to escape the oppressions, cruelties, and cold weather of the East Coast. We look like your ancestors, but we try not to act the way you do.

We are a culture of refugees, I among them, who left home and town and job and church looking for a better life. Several kinds of creatures made the westward move. There were crippled spirits who would do well nowhere, but who could do no worse than to stay where they were. There were dreamers who were sure that what was wrong was in New York rather than in themselves, who find themselves with their backs to the Pacific Ocean, no place left to go but despair; they help account for San Francisco's being the national capital of alcoholism and suicide. There were boom followers, con artists dedicated to the exploitation of everybody, the fast-buck boys who make trends instead of traditions. There were exhibitionists who wanted to be stars and have their feet set in Hollywood concrete. There were wanderers who saw California as a fertile crescent curving around a coast with room and space and time. And there were pioneers who wanted to escape the manifest density of Boston, Washington, Philadelphia, and New York for the purpose of taking a new existence in their own hands.

What all the American refugees had in common was optimism, well founded or not. They ripped up their roots and risked transplanting.

They are not the same sort of people they left behind, nor are they like the men and women in the middle of the United States. This book is about both extremes: the lives at the ends of America and how they exist against each other. The coasts control what happens in between; East may be East and West may be West, but hardly anybody parachutes down over Chicago. One social theorist suggested picking up a flat map of the United States and curving it into a column so that the two coasts touch—a truer picture of the country, with the two joined surfaces representing the wealth, power, and future of the continent.

But the meeting ground is not smooth. The flat beaches of Long Island have little in common with the craggy shore of Big Sur, and the citizens who comb both coasts are rarely searching for the same pleasures.

A Canadian architect thinks that the northern half of the Western Hemisphere should have been divided longitudinally, not latitudinally. One country would have included Montreal, Ottawa, New York, Washington, and Miami. Another would have embraced Toronto, Chicago, and St. Louis. The western nation would have Vancouver, Seattle, San Francisco, and Los Angeles between its borders. The idea was that European tradition absorbs the East, industrial muscle dominates the middle, and hedonism conquers the West. Some facts of life sustain his argument.

A more important argument is that California can be killed by its East Coast ancestors.

The facts of modern American life are that power, money, and the media continue to live in the old country—especially New York City and Washington, D.C. If the West is the center of pleasure, the East remains the center of gravity, where the federal government and the financial gurus decide for the rest of us. The publishers and the television and radio networks are back there, too, determining what's fit to read and watch, deciding what descriptions are appropriate as mirrors held before the mass audience of Everywhere.

The East was what gave California its national reputation for sexual acrobatics, lotus eating, religious frenzy, ridiculous taste, and a fad for every fruit tree. Those were the silly years, when the West was treated as a show-business joke or a shaggy-dog story.

The East was what also tried to change the American mind after California grew up to become the most populous state in the Union. Easterners, always numbed by numbers, suddenly sat up in 1960 to see that California would have more Congressmen, more taxpayers, and more technology than New York. There would have to be a new dictum: Take the West seriously instead of sillily. Books and magazines began to describe California as THE TEST BED FOR TOMORROW, THE WINDOW ON THE FUTURE, THE LABORATORY FOR THE NEXT AMERICAN LIFE.

Some of us refugees have been furious ever since. Here were our parents still telling us what we would be when we grew up. We had left home, renounced roots, revolted against old aspirations, and yet they were still trying to be the dominant influences in our lives—with the affluence and arrogance to get away with it. If being treated as silly or childish was annoying, being treated as the the face of the future was a goddamn burden.

California never wanted to be treated too seriously. California never asked for the westward tilt —especially if the tilt came from body count, not clout. Part of this book is about people who want to be left alone, people who went west for privacy, people who don't want to be told by outsiders who they are or what they're about.

California has no intention of living up to what Easterners expect of it.

California resents being spoken for rather than speaking for itself. (You will, naturally, notice that this book is brought to you through the courtesy and sponsorship of an Eastern publisher. But the opinions expressed herein are strictly those of the refugee writer, a man who was born and raised on the East Coast, who doesn't miss what he left behind, who doesn't much care if he never sees the East Coast again.)

California admits that the concentration of American might is on the opposite shore. So please stop trying to parent us and pat us on the head because of your false set of values about numbers.

California doesn't necessarily need to be under-

stood, and California certainly doesn't expect Easterners to understand. If a rebellious child figures his
parents will one day wake up and applaud his behavior,
then he probably won't resort to running away. Americans ran to California because they had no such hopes.

The thesis is that East and West do not sustain the
same sort of citizens. The differences in style, love,
politics, mobility, business, urbanity, amusements,
and mental health will be examined in the chapters
that follow.

The fear that impels the chapters that follow wells
up from a need to preserve those differences. The people of the Pacific do not want to be pacified into pale
New Yorkers, into living behind a continuous glass
curtain/wall of high-rises, into accepting the urban
patterns that made them leave in the first place.

The bedrock argument is that we coexist on each
coast with two prototypical populations. On the West
are the immature, the experimenters, the adventurers,
the non-belongers, and, yes, the provincials who are
pleased to be in the provinces. On the East are the
adults, the synthesizers, the stabilizers, the club
members, and the power mongers who wanted to stay
where the purse strings are.

When I meet Eastern envoys, they habitually want
to know how a person can be happy so far removed
from "the theater," the galleries, the French restaurants, the brahmins of Park Avenue, the board rooms of
Madison Avenue, and the commerce of Fifth Avenue.
The question isn't really that. What they want to know
is whether a Californian doesn't feel lost and unloved
so far from the apron of mother country. New Yorkers
rarely go to the theater, anyway. They were locked in

7

long before they bought the bolts and barriers to protect them from crime in the streets.

East Coast people have their own fears, and those fears are real, in terms of the violence bred by density. Easterners are afraid of straying too far from the neighborhood that nurtured them. New York futurist Alvin Toffler recently asked, "But what do you do at night in Los Angeles?" Telling him about our own theater or San Francisco's opera seemed unnecessary. If I had said we do more doping and screwing and nude encountering than East Side East Coast people, he probably would have been satisfied—and smug in the comfort that his entertainments are more exalted than those of the provinces. But what I did say was that Californians do nothing and do everything at night; they merely make fewer reservations.

Just as the colonists seemed crude and vulgar compared to the elite of London, Californians are indeed brash in comparison to their relatives along the Atlantic. California optimism is extremely important and an element of the brashness Californians are afraid of losing.

My first impression, fifteen years ago, when I was fresh from the elbow pokes of Manhattan, was of California friendliness. I met it wherever I sought service: at modest restaurants, at the gasoline pumps, at supermarket checkout stands. The people who waited on other people in the West were uncommonly cordial. What in the beginning seemed a noble character trait later seemed more of a sales approach. The servers in Southern California were waiting to be discovered.

The Lana Turner legend was not lost upon them, the illusion that a person could sit on a soda-fountain stool in a two-scoop sweater and be found for film stardom. Not all the supermarket checkers and car parkers wanted to be in movies, but they carried a real hope of advancement into their daily routines. You, the customer, could be the agent of their good fortune—if not you, then maybe the next person waiting for service, or the one after, or the one after that. The friendliness had a strong element of opportunism about it, each server rehearsing his or her act of warmth, to be ready for the big break at the end of the hose holding the regular gas.

Opportunism did not diminish the cordiality, however. And the smiling business exchanges of California made commerce happier for all concerned. The contrast with New York was chilling. I used to walk behind what I called the Saks-for-lunch bunch on Fifth Avenue, eavesdropping on their loneliness and frustration. The bunch was a group of women, interchangeable, from hundreds of offices, each of them wanting more from a job or men or chance than was likely to happen. They ate tuna-salad sandwiches at their desks in order to be free for the hour-long window-shopping expedition on the boulevard. The bunch rarely bought anything; being at Saks was luxury by association.

Those women were happy compared to Eastern store clerks and waiters and subway conductors. New York service was and is terrible, because the servers are bitter people who expect to spend the rest of their employable days doing the same dreary things, hearing the same hurry-up orders, dodging the same pushers and shovers. And, alas, they are right. Nothing better is about to happen their way. The East is a stratified place in which citizens stay in their places. Optimism doesn't live there beyond early adulthood. In New York, working people expect the worst, and usually they are rewarded by it. In California, working people expect to move ahead, and often they do.

This book could be a recruiting device if I'm not careful. If my argument convinces one more American to move west, then it will have failed ingloriously. California needs a new immigration explosion about as much as a new earthquake boom. The West could be killed if the mother-country parents ran right after the runaways and tried to settle in the sprawls of San Francisco and San Diego.

The states of Oregon and Washington appreciated the problem ahead of California. The James G. Blaine Society of Oregon has spent decades trying to persuade Easterners and Californians that they'd be unhappy in the rugged majesty of Coos Bay or Klamath Falls; Governor Tom McCall made anti-immigration an official state policy. DON'T CALIFORNICATE OREGON, say the bumper stickers. Washington has a semi-serious organization called Lesser Seattle which fights booms and boosterism whether business is good or bad. People in the Northwest saw what was coming to California, and they began erecting semi-polite propaganda barricades against us and against our East Coast kin.

The Lesser Los Angeles organization was not born until 1970, almost too late for California's good. But it became a kind of model for municipal modesty in the West, underlining our fear of bringing another East to western shores. Lesser Los Angeles attracted more than six thousand members in the first months of its being. But it had no dues, no meetings, no officers, no agenda,

10

no brochures, and no active program. Such a negative stance was perfectly in keeping with a group that claimed growth was no good, and with personal characteristics of Californians, who resent making financial contributions, dislike attending meetings, distrust elected officials, and generally hold their privacy above programs. Lesser Los Angeles only sported buttons and bumper stickers to communicate a frame of mind. Californians, captives of their cars, often speak to each other with slogans just above their rear exhausts.

Earthquake, aerospace layoffs, and smog accomplished more than Lesser Los Angeles in muffling the boom. The instabilities of California were becoming clear. The early seventies saw a dramatic drop in arriving American refugees. And many of us breathed secret sighs of pleasure, feeling less threatened by the East.

What we didn't reckon with was the energy crisis of 1974. Suddenly the prospect of inflation plus unemployment was everywhere in America. Later I'll come to a scenario about how a new boom might begin in California, fused by a critical shortage of home heating fuel, set in motion by a below-zero winter in the East, and finally exploded by a population that has lost faith in its own future—if American life is terrible, why not at least go where it is warm while it is terrible? The boom hasn't happened yet; the winters of '73 and '74 were, happily, not as cold as normal, and Eastern people could stay with their comforting notions about smog being the most noxious poison in America.

But I still worry about maintaining the distance between me and my more mature brethren on the East Coast. Many of these remarks, therefore, will be unflattering to and about Californians. I would like to present us honestly rather than favorably. Some of our virtues can be seen as ugly flaws. Our attitude of live-and-let-live often may breed lack of responsibility. Our love of privacy may be defined, fairly, as insularity; our physical freedom as debauchery; our obsession with health as hypochondria; even our optimism as simple ignorance.

I will acknowledge that we wouldn't exist if it weren't for the East Coast. That's both a compliment and a complaint. California is a response to and a reaction against the country that spawned it. California's instability is caused by occasional acts of God and frequent acts of women and men.

Let us begin to approach the peculiar people of the West by looking at the people who pretend not to be there: the visible Californians who refuse to be approachable Californians.

-II-

Non-Working Numbers

California breeds a personal maverick I've learned to recognize as the unlisted man (or the unlisted person, as women begin to assert unidentity along with identity).

The unlisted person seeks unapproachability by insulation, guarding name and address and telephone number from as much of the outside world as possible.

Easterners tend to think of unlisted telephones as a sort of snobbery rather than as self-protection. They are wrong. The unlisted Californian is interested more in being unreachable than in being fashionable. Apparently, the psychological need comes from the impulse to refugee flight already discussed. While it is undeniably true that Californians are only the amalgam of Texans, Iowans, New Jerseyites, and New Yorkers—the mixed-up sum of the American parts—it is also true that they are no longer the same as the people they left behind. Californians may retain identity with their old countries, but they are the renegade side of the original families. They threw away as much old baggage as they took with them. They came west to find themselves by losing themselves.

So California is the unlisted capital of the world, with more people who choose not to appear in the white pages than anywhere else.

George Peppard is a typical example of the show-business celebrity who doesn't want to hear from strangers. You will not find George's name in the Beverly Hills phone book. You probably wouldn't expect to, because we have all grown up with the idea that actors must be elusive. But if you were persistent or devious, if you had access to Celebrity Service or to one of Peppard's agents, you might be able to discover George's unlisted phone number. That would not mean that you had penetrated to his person. Having the number of an unlisted person is only an entry into the first layer of insulation.

Invariably, an answering service is the second layer. Most celebrities never answer the first telephone they had installed in their homes. Never. If you called George's number, you would be answered by a polite male at a service a few miles away from the Peppard household. He would do one of several things, depending upon who you were and what you said you wanted. If he recognized you as a friend or associate of Peppard's, he would call George on the second, more secret phone, and if Peppard wanted to talk to you, the answerer would tie the two secret lines together. If he was unsure about your business or your motive, the answerer would likely tell you that Peppard was un-reachable at the moment but that the message would be forwarded. The answering service performs as a remote receptionist, with all the oral weapons a receptionist can employ: "out of town," "in a meeting," "unavailable."

The phone the service itself uses to reach Peppard is the third layer of insulation. George may ignore it if he chooses to, secure in the knowledge that all intrusions by the outside world will be noted on small pieces of paper piled up for his later reference.

Such complicated efforts to protect oneself extend beyond show business to medicine to law to affluent Californians in all occupations. And all of us have learned to expect some difficulty in making contact with other creatures; the odd paradox is that the better known a person is, the less public that person becomes. The more familiar the face, the more fugitive its wearer.

What may surprise the larger audience is the amount of unlisting at the opposite end of the economic ladder. About as many poor Californians unlist themselves as wealthy Californians. The desire to avoid contact is strongest in poverty neighborhoods and prestige neighborhoods, leaving the middle class the most accessible section of California society.

Television, of all omnipotent forces, unearthed this peculiar phenomenon. The people who make soap and cereal, obsessed with reaching people through advertising messages, use rating services to discover whether their messages are being delivered to the maximum number of watching bodies. Television entertainment lives or dies on the basis of whether it helps sell the sponsors' wares. And the sponsors make life/death decisions based on ratings, assuming that the more homes penetrated by a particular program, the more soap that program is likely to sell. Most of the rating work has been done by telephone, either by massive programs of direct calls to viewers or by monitoring samples of viewers.

In the early seventies, the validity of the samples' composition was challenged by ad agencies and by TV executives themselves, who argued that the top 20 percent and the bottom 20 percent of the population were not represented in most ratings results. The raters were surveying only the middle 60 percent of the people, and that distorted the picture of people's preferences. The quite rich and the quite poor do not have the same tastes as the members of the middle. Even the most bragged-about dubious achievement of American television—"giving the people what they want"—was suddenly in question. Television knew what the middle wanted; it had almost no idea what was wanted in the ghettos of either extreme, because their residents lived unlisted lives.

Poor people's reasons for being unlisted are akin to those of the rich. The poor don't want to be bothered with requests, with pests asking for rent or overdue time payments—or for television preferences, either. Poor people have learned, through human scuffle, that the more available you are, the more it costs you.

Californians have fewer locks on their doors than Easterners do, but they have more devices for preserving anonymity.

The unlisted address is a relatively new refinement of the unlisted person. Some Westerners want to be accessible to the outside world without ever being visited by it. I confess to being one of these insulated hybrids. My number is in the telephone book, because I haven't figured out a way to pretend to play journalist without allowing day-to-day exposure to strangers. But the house number at which that telephone number lives is omitted. It looks, in the phone book, as if the writer might have ears and mouth but no body.

My excuse for being only partly there is an incident that happened about ten years ago. Two men arrived at the house late one Sunday night, claiming to want to talk about a story. (These were more innocent years—or, at least, I was more innocent.) I let them in, and they were more interested in the two children about to go to bed than they were in any news event. I felt stupid. I learned the next week that one of them had a remarkable record with the police for child molesting. (He later died of an asthma attack during a political demonstration.) I learned to guard against unwanted visitors, simply by removing my address from the telephone book.

While we Californians are less friendly about being at home, we are usually quite available at the office, especially compared to East Coast business people. Reaching a corporate president or board chairman by phone is not at all remarkable in the West. Some of them even answer their own calls, not wanting a secretary as interceptor. I remember, for instance, reaching the boss of Western Airlines one day without passing through a Person Friday or an executive assistant. The experience is so simple as to be unnerving.

This may be an example of the way Californians

tend to think of serious work as merely a means toward serious play, saving their most strenuous efforts for private leisure. Talking to a New York executive or a Washington bureaucrat during the working day is never easy—sometimes advance appointments must be made for mere telephone calls—but talking to them at home is often as easy as dialing their listed numbers. The reverse is true in the West. The California executive is on call at the office. Just don't try to interrupt him or her when away from the working desk.

But as the world becomes more peopled, more people on both coasts are inclined to resist being reachable. In the spring of 1973 I asked a class of UCLA graduate journalism students to make contact with a variety of supposedly important people: actors and university regents and tycoons and political leaders. I wanted them to know the frustration of trying to establish communication in a culture that wallows in ways to communicate. The students did not do well, nor did they have a happy time. They did discover, in the course of ringing resistance, several facts of unlisted life.

If a student called an important person and simply announced his or her name, the important person almost never picked up the telephone.

If a student called and said he or she was working on a graduate project at UCLA, the odds on response improved slightly. If a student said he or she was "with" UCLA, the odds improved more. If a student used a friend to play bogus secretary, the chances of connection increased further; the bogus secretary reached the important person's secretary and introduced the caller as someone with the university

—obviously someone important enough to have his or her own line of communications defense. Once again, the rules of the game are ridiculous: The more important one is, the more unimportant people one needs to speak in one's behalf.

The UCLA students also learned the code for non-communicators. If a secretary said the important person was out of town, that meant there was little chance that the important person would ever return the call. If the important person was said to be in a meeting, there was a possibility that the important person was potentially reachable in a day or two, if the caller was persistent. If the important person was said to be willing to return the call, there were two opposite possibilities: One, that the call would indeed be returned; two, that, by taking the initiative, the important person could avoid communication forever.

My own experience with both coasts indicates that more calls are returned in New York and Washington, D.C., than they are in San Francisco and Los Angeles. The East honors the formalities, although often the person assigned to return calls is an underling who maintains courtesy without facilitating communications. The West is more accessible at work, but sloppier: Messages are taken, forwarded, and then thrown away without anyone's deigning to answer the original request.

We have perfected other devious ways to postpone telephone contact in California, using electronics or a secretary as a shield. One is to accept no messages until the end of the working day. Another is to pretend to receive a long-distance call on another line as soon as a conversation has begun; Californians are attuned to

19

the idea that a call from the East takes precedence over anything that might be said between two Westerners. A third method is to return all calls during the lunch hour. If one can return a call with reasonable certainty that the original caller isn't there, then two objectives may be achieved with one ploy: Honor is upheld, and a message has been left that the callee tried to reach the caller; action has been put off, because the two parties haven't spoken, and, with good luck, nothing will ever have to be done or decided, because by the time the original caller calls back again, the problem may have gone away.

Charles Webb, the author of *The Graduate,* had one of the most sophisticated systems of all for appearing to uphold honor while avoiding humankind. Of course, he was unlisted. His next line of defense was an electronic box standing next to the telephone. When an unwanted creature crept through on the unlisted line, Webb turned on the box, which emitted a terrible squawk and drowned out both parties. Webb screamed apologies, blamed the telephone system, and asked the other party to call back immediately, whereupon he reactivated the box and shouted that there was obviously something so wrong with his phone that it would be impossible to talk until the phone company had sent a repairperson.

What the reclusive writer, at the bottom of his soul, couldn't stand was the casual friendliness of the West. Webb considered himself something of an artist, and he resented the way Westerners intruded on one another. He finally moved to a bucolic corner of New England to avoid returning the calls of California.

Other artists have made the opposite move, coming to Southern California precisely because they thought they could be more alone in the West than in the East. Most Los Angeles residents don't even know that Arnold Schoenberg, Igor Stravinsky, Thomas Mann, and Aldous Huxley once made conscious decisions to live in Southern California. Most Los Angeles residents wouldn't care if they did know. And some Los Angeles residents have never heard of these artists anyway. That was the attraction for artists in the first place. They wanted to live in a place where they could go about their creative, singular, lonely business.

The East, especially New York, has some of the qualities of colony found in Paris and London. Painters tend to hang out in one neighborhood or one bistro and compare techniques, passions, statements. Theater people in the East have their own closed cocktail circuits. Writers have theirs. Composers have theirs. Incest in the arts is a European custom carried over to the older side of America. The artist who likes to belong to a school likes to live in New York, where there is a kind of collective loyalty, or paranoia, and a kind of mutually nourished inspiration.

The artist who finds feeding on other artists self-destructive tends to want to be absorbed in a place where he or she won't be noticed. Los Angeles does not have cafés where composers and writers congregate. Artists in Southern California don't maintain their own asylums; they do or die in the same bedlam that houses other residents. They do not seek birds of similar feather, and they do not require social exposure at cocktail parties or charity receptions.

The serious Southern California artist is delighted to have the amusement business as an added protection

21

against the sins of celebrity. California natives and tourists alike make a game out of seeing stars, or at least their homes. Maps of movie star's homes are still a staple business of the boulevards; people continue to buy charts showing where the celebrities are supposed to live, or once lived. A community that adores the popular idols offers protection for more profound spirits.

Gregor Piatigorsky and Jascha Heifetz have lived happily in Los Angeles for decades. Both have taught at the University of Southern California. Both have performed at the Los Angeles County Music Center. Both have managed to remain private figures.

Of the pair, Piatigorsky is the more social animal. He makes occasional appearances in the society pages and the fund-raising circles.

Heifetz is almost a recluse, almost the apotheosis of the solitary artist sitting in splendid isolation. He has two houses, both unlisted. One is in the hills above Beverly Hills. The other is along the beach at Malibu. Heifetz has some of the same insulation as George Peppard, who lives below him. If one penetrates the first unlisted layer and dials Heifetz's home, one never reaches him directly.

Only twice in my California memory has the septuagenarian violinist lent himself to a non-musical community cause. During the sixties Heifetz, appalled at smog, built himself an electric-powered automobile and allowed himself to be photographed as an example of what an environmentally concerned citizen could do in California without sacrificing the mobility of private transportation. Heifetz, appalled at the California confusion in human services, was willing to talk to the press about the need for one emergency telephone number that would respond to calls for police fire, department, and emergency medical care. Heifetz is himself a victim of the odd overlapping of jurisdiction in Southern California. His unlisted hilltop self has a Beverly Hills post office and telephone exchange but a Los Angeles legal address. Mail is delivered from Beverly Hills. Garbage is picked up by Los Angeles, which also provides police and fire protection. Several years ago Heifetz realized how difficult it was for a resident to know where to yell for help. There are nearly eighty cities in Los Angeles County. There are many unincorporated areas which contract for health, education, police, and fire services. Sometimes the nearest fire station is not the one that can respond to a call. Sometimes property and lives are lost because a person in the midst of emergency can't tell which listed emergency service serves where.

Heifetz joined a community push for an emergency number that would tie into all services into all jurisdictions. Such a universal number, 911 on the dial, has already been successfully installed in several megalopolitan areas, including New York.

Heifetz came down off his hill to lobby government, through the media and among influential people. The unlisted virtuoso discovered that the telephone company could make the necessary technical installations. But politicians did not make the necessary legislation. Jealousies between heads of service agencies became pressures on the local elected officials. One department didn't want another to have easy access to its records on response times, reaction procedures, and mistakes made. Proprietary insecuri-

23

ties were more important than people served, it seemed. Besides, 911 was expensive to establish. And some chiefs argued that 911, in practice, added one more layer of insulation between the caller and the agency. Heifetz was angry. He couldn't understand why New York, with all its chaos, should have a better system of serving immediate needs than Southern California. I could. California's unlisted man is normally not his brother's keeper. The West won't have 911 until the end of the seventies.

J. D. Salinger, the most celebrated reclusive writer in America, surprised me many years ago when he hid out in New Hampshire; I would have thought him more at home in California with the other famous fugitives. Ray Bradbury is the only serious writer I know in Southern California who maintains a large public presence and a large private following. Bradbury likes to surround himself with other authors to talk out the troubles of their trade. Unlike Christopher Isherwood. Unlike Ariel and Will Durant. Unlike Irving Stone. Even unlike Irving Wallace.

The visual artists of California also keep to themselves, and avoid mixing with each other as conscientiously as they avoid talk shows on television. Ed Kienholz, a sculptor absorbed with life and death, is another example of the disappearing celebrity. Kienholz is better known in Europe now than in America, probably better known in America than in his old neighborhood above Hollywood. For years Kienholz sat in the hills with his hunting dogs and hunting guns high above the galleries on La Cienega Boulevard. He always preferred poker openings to museum openings.

Kienholz is also a symbol of what this book is about. Just before the turn of the seventies, Kienholz started building himself a mammoth log cabin near Hope, Idaho. By hand. With rough timber. Without subcontractors.

California, he had decided, had become too crowded. People were poaching on his privacy. Too much density, too many demands, too little peace. Kienholz claimed to have once loved California, but now it was becoming an unreasonable facsimile of New York. So he would make another home in the West, on the shores of Lake Pend Oreille, where the outdoors were still out there. He would insulate himself by geography.

The Durants, Will and Ariel, who came from the East Coast, are a better example of coping in California. These historians have used a whole half century to chronicle the saga of human life. Their *Story of Civilization* is the most ambitious interpretation of the species ever attempted. The first volume appeared in 1935, and subsequent volumes were published through the forties, fifties, and sixties.

The Durants have done almost all of it in one house not far from Kienholz's old house in the hills. They have rarely chosen to leave long-ago history for everyday Hollywood, preferring to examine the world that was rather than the world that is, in almost total privacy.

I was once doing a survey of celebrities to record their favorite places in California—for scenery, for vacationing, for weather. The Durants politely declined to participate. Back came a letter saying they hadn't seen California; because they had been so busy for so many years looking over their shoulders, they'd hardly had a chance to step out of their house.

California gave them what the East couldn't: shelter from the contemporary. The indoor climate of the West Coast is what gave them protection from the hostility of the outside and the glare of publicity.

We do not drop in in the West. Our social lives are our most scheduled lives, because we honor each other's seclusion to an extraordinary degree. We may dress less formally in California, we may call each other by first names with automatic arrogance, and we may suffer mate-swapping nightclubs as a sign of our sophistication, but we do not visit friends uninvited.

When I lived in Boston, my neighbors, quite proper in all ways, never thought twice about dropping in for an evening. When I lived in a New York suburb, I once defined a garden apartment as a commune where a neighbor could appear in his undershirt on your lawn any weekend day. When I stayed on the Main Line outside Philadelphia, the most refined citizens made random raids on one another if they happened to be passing by.

Nobody in California ever seems to be passing by, for one thing. Training on the freeways tends to promote tunnel vision; we have a mentality focused on singular destinations over vast distances.

The pedestrian remains a rarity in residential areas (unless the pedestrian is attached to a poodle). Californians do not meander down to the local pub or the school playground. They drive.

We do not drop in, essentially, because we continue to assume that a person's leisure time is the most sacred time of all.

Instead, we have parties. Home dinner parties are a California staple from Sausalito to San Diego. Big dinner parties are *big*, involving caterers and rented tents and hired car parkers and even living decorations. Weather, I suppose, makes such celebrations seem extravagant by East Coast standards. A pancake-house mogul, for instance, once decided to dump live swans in his swimming pool as a footnote to an outdoor festivity. He had the birds tinted to match the rest of the rented decorations: one blue swan, one gold. Guests were invited to blend in with the environment by wearing the same colors. The food, the costumes, the set decorations were superb. But the swans were unnerved, either by the noise or by their newly dyed feathers. They came out of the pool to attack, biting blue suede shoes and pecking gold-sprayed hairdos. The poor birds' trainer finally had to bind the swans' feet to keep them in their watery place.

The big home dinner parties, carefully scored and scripted, do have a debt to show business. I remember one election-night event produced by Sylvia and Irving Wallace a few years ago. Irving writes popular novels; he also writes painstakingly researched novels. He's a cordial man. And conscientious. The first surprise of the evening was at the door, where a couple of attractive women were standing at the entry with a name tag for each guest. Name tags at a home dinner. We looked like a convention, which is hardly conventional for a crowd of supposed friends.

The second surprise, to complement the first, was a book: a printed brochure with all our names in it.

Following each name was a job description, such as "Norman Lear . . . producer," "Lorne Greene . . . actor," "Judd Marmor . . . psychiatrist." Now all of us good friends could recognize one another, if not on sight, God forbid, then surely by quick reference to our private program. We could look one another up. We could immediately know what sort of small talk might suit what sort of guest. The women's movement was only beginning in California in 1970; as I recall, most of the women at that dinner were described by what their husbands did—supporting players for the party. But it was an astonishing experience for a couple of hundred unlisted people to wear their names on their chests and to be part of a cast directory.

That's one of the things we do at night, Alvin Toffler. I'm sure you may find it bizarre, if not barbaric. But it's also innocent. It avoids the terrible talk about "And what do *you* do," and it's a sort of leveling device when the big names and the no names all have the same size credit printed on their persons.

The big home dinner parties are in lieu of drop-ins and having to repay social debts with a long series of small parties. My friends Nancy and Art Manella may also seem strange by Eastern standards. They like to travel and take pictures. They do not like to cook. Two or three times a year the Manellas have large slide-show parties about wherever they have been last: India, North Africa, the Soviet Union. They are good photographers, fortunately. Nancy is a good narrator, having had previous experience as a musuem docent and a television newsperson. They both have an eye for anthropological detail and architectural nuance. The Manella screenings are always learning experiences.

But the hosts avoid the kitchen without calling caterers. Their friends the Rachmans like to cook. The Rachmans come to all the parties as honored guests and galley slaves. They do a good turn in the kitchen, and then they come out to be with the other couples. The Manellas thereby preserve the aura of a casual party and their separation from the ovens.

Joyce Haber, the movie columnist, has built a portion of her career in categorizing guest lists from A to B. "A" guests are the people everyone would like to have identified with their homes. "B" guests are smaller celebrities, reeled in if the bigger fish are taking other party bait. Sometimes A and B guests are simultaneously at the same affair. Sometimes they are segregated at the same affair. Haber herself once had the courage to have two halves of one party. The A guests were invited to a private film screening in the den following a handsome dinner in the dining room. The B guests were invited only to the screening. They were scheduled a couple of hours after the A guests were asked to come. The B's were invited to enter through the garage, then they wouldn't have to watch the A's getting up from dinner. By such front- and door gambits, California unlisteds manage to measure their social standings.

The home screening, incidentally, is a major amusement in the amusement industry. The wealthiest producers, directors, and actors have their own theaters built into their houses. They have access to their own movies before release to the paying public, and trade them through what is called the "Bel-Air Circuit," graciously allowing one another the privilege of criticism ahead of the reviewers. The private movie party spares insulated celebrities from having to show face—and possibly lose face—at a general trade screening or sneak preview.

California has one more kind of party more often than the East: the charity or fund-raising event held at a private home instead of a hotel. The idea is that somebody's residence is that body's most cherished preserve, and such intimacy will raise more money for the cause than would a rental hall. The cause doesn't have to pay for use of the premises. The house itself is often a showplace which lures contributors out of curiosity. The ambience is more amiable, making stingy people less comfortable about pledging small amounts. The food can be bought at wholesale prices.

Political parties love to stage house parties in Southern California. So do social movements, medical charities, universities, and private secondary schools.

Ramsey Clark, the former Attorney General, was the guest of honor at such a party when he was running for U.S. Senator from New York.

Nobody thought there was anything odd about a candidate from New York coming to Sunset Boulevard for a fund-raising event. The two coasts are now quite used to using each other. Jess Unruh campaigned in New York when he was running for governor of California in 1970. Robert Kennedy campaigned in California when he was running for senator from New York in 1964. Power and money live at both ends of the nation.

What was odd was Clark's speech in the Sunset setting. The liberal lawyer was talking about taking government back from big business, about how the people could no longer afford to let their candidates be bought by the big contributors, about how we could reform the democratic process only by eliminating the big lobbyists and the hold they have over big legislators.

He was standing in front of a glass wall that looked out over the green lawns of the Los Angeles Country Club, a lush backyard that stretched to infinity.

He was talking about the need for Americans to cut their conspicuous consumption and stop blighting a crowded universe.

He was standing next to a mammoth pool table, in the playroom adjoining the living room.

He was talking about saving energy and no longer relying on the restraint of the multinational oil producers or the whims of Middle East monarchies. But his entire audience had arrived by car. All of us had come in small groups of two or three. We were sitting in the lap of squander while Clark lectured on the squalor in so much of the outside world.

Some opulent Southern California homes are specifically designed to house parties rather than people. Like the pool, the tennis court, and the sauna, the house has to have a huge room where folding chairs can be set up for a fund-raiser. One home in Trousdale Estates has survived a series of liberal causes. The owners are usually absent, having at last become bored by their own appetite for generosity. Party givers replace one another night after night, peace yielding to amnesty yielding to ecology yielding to the UN. Some group always has the floor.

The Southern California unlisted people have a reputation for leaving early. The reputation is deserved. If the most public figures have the most private insulation, they also have a fetish for going home before there's any chance for hilarity.

The routine, run-of-the-A-list party begins at seven P.M. Dinner is served at eight. Brandy is offered, but rarely drunk, at ten. Guests start to leave for home at eleven. The most famous guests are usually the first to go, enjoying a kind of escape perquisite based on the presumption of business and impatience. "Impatience" is the proper word, I think. Important people go home when they have nothing important to offer. They'd rather be in bed than not be entertaining.

San Franciscans do not behave quite that way, so the elusive habit must have started in the movie business. In the old days, when almost all the shooting was outdoors, movie people had to catch the dawn, and casting calls were for as early as six A.M. But shooting styles have changed, and there aren't that many movies being made any more, anyway. I think the quick exits have more to do with insulated people not wanting to expose their persons in anything but extremely limited engagements. California leisure, remember, is a serious business. We all need the sleep.

And, of course, California sleep causes California dreaming.

-III-

Out of Place, Out of Mind

California dreaming is daydreaming and nightdreaming; is expectations in San Mateo or Bloomington, Indiana; is the illusion that if a man is what he eats, then a man and woman are also where they are, that place changes lives; is the ultimate disillusionment when things go wrong and a person finds that place is where your back is against the Pacific Ocean with no room left to improvise and no geographies to blame.

"Maybe . . . ," he said, hesitating before forming the next words, "if we had gone to Salt Lake or Denver back in the early sixties instead of Santa Barbara, things would have been different. What we created here for our children was an idyllic lotus land. An unreal pastoral existence. Things are so easy in Southern California for the children. So languid."

Those are the words of William Loud, told to Jon

Nordheimer of *The New York Times* in the spring of 1974. Loud, you'll remember, was the father in the twelve-part psycho-documentary on National Educational Television, *The American Family.*

No accident that a national search for a supposedly representative American family finally homed in on Santa Barbara, a beautiful slice of shore between San Francisco and Los Angeles where the oil slick met the sea. Santa Barbara is almost the epitome of the California dream: a city so small and rich that it can afford to discriminate against industry, a natural frame of mountains to contain a voluptuous curve of coastline, a community that collects and conserves and attracts think tanks, because even intellectuals like to play tennis on a year-round basis.

No accident, either, that producer Craig Gilbert was from New York. Gilbert had come to California for NET several times, to do various programs on culture. This time he was looking for culture as lived rather than culture as performed in California. He wanted a family that seemed to be the quintessence of comfortable life, where there were children and aspirations and feelings of continuity. He wasn't trying to do a *Winesburg, Ohio* on television, in which families hid their sins behind respectable hometown façades. I remember meeting Gilbert one day before the filming had started. He was elated by the Louds. He knew they had troubles, but he also knew they had intelligence and the peculiar California candor that would allow him to poke a camera into the private portions of their lives. Once unlocked, unlisted people really open up. The series was not supposed to be sensational; it was intended to be intimate.

34

The results were intimate all right, even devastating. Bill and Pat broke up their marriage for a national audience. Son Lance told the country he was gay and wanted to be a rock star. The four other Loud children became examples of American television celebrities, people famous for nothing so much as being themselves.

Whether television exposure was a cause of the rupture or whether television only happened to be there when the inevitable occurred was an argument of interminable delight on the Carson and Cavett shows. What was equally interesting was Bill Loud's willingness to blame television in general and the state of California for what happened to his family. While he was telling Nordheimer about languidity being a basis for family failure, his friend Cheri McCarthy was saying that things would have been no different elsewhere.

"Yes they would," continued Loud. "If I had to do it all over again, I'd beat hell out of those kids and throw their goddamn television sets into the Pacific. TV gave them a completely unreal picture of the world."

TV, answered McCarthy with unassailable logic, would have been the same in Salt Lake or Denver. But it was where the TV was that turned out to be Loud's complaint, and he was saying life wouldn't have been the same in a colder reality:

"At least they would have had to put shoes on to go outdoors. At least make that effort. God, when we came to California I thought it would be like Andy Hardy in Beverly Hills, with Patty like some motherlike figure like Ann Rutherford, and we'd just play tennis and swim all the time. God, up in Oregon we were all huddled up for months just to avoid the rain."

Funny about Oregon, which is where the Louds lived before they moved to Santa Barbara and national prominence. Oregon is now to California what this book is to the East Coast: a shout for being left alone. Recent Oregon governor Tom McCall made a habit of inviting Californians to visit his state but not stay there. He was complaining in 1974 that eighteen thousand Californians a year were moving to Oregon, while few Oregonians ever considered making the opposite move. The Oregon prejudice is that boom breeds density and density breeds a decline and fall of living quality—a prejudice that twentieth-century development tends to support.

But Santa Barbara is less dense than Portland, and Loud wasn't blaming urban misery for his troubles. Quite the opposite, in fact:

"Southern California was like the answer to everyone's dreams. Frankly, our country-club values are shlock values. The California dream is a shlock dream. If you ever want to see some bored people, take a look at sex orgies. I've made the Long Beach swingles scene and done it on an eight-to-one basis twice in the past couple of years, and it's a lot of bored people, and those are the values California gives our kids."

Loud's leap from languidness to sex orgies is a non sequitur of sorts, but it does give some credence to the thesis that sex is a serious business in California. Leisure isn't taken lightly. And his whole thesis about what went wrong in beautiful Santa Barbara is an echo of older American guilt. Life was not supposed to be comfortable. Climate was supposed to be harsh. Pleas-

36

ure was temporary and earned by hard work. Pleasure was not for everyday, not something you interrupted occasionally for the office. To live the California dream with style, you must invert all that old guilt. Loud couldn't.

"Shlock" is not the word for Loud's argument against the dream. The trouble is that most Americans were never trained to live with the dream if it ever came true. It's one thing to talk about sailing off Sausalito or skiing at Mount Shasta or even golfing in San Diego on an everyday basis, but it's quite another exercise to act out such fantasies. Americans' inability to retire gracefully is connected to disillusion with the California dream. Most of our countrymen are incapable of enjoying free time in perpetuity, even after they've worked until sixty-five to earn it. The Puritan ethic not only gets in the way, it leaves us as adults who've never acquired the knack of being blissfully lazy. We don't define laziness in some of its proper terms: contemplation, tranquility, rest. And we aren't good at it anyway. The hard-working ant and the busy beaver are model animals for American schoolchildren. The graceful porpoise, one of nature's most intelligent creatures, was never celebrated until recently, because it didn't perform any industrial chores such as building towns or dams.

Most Americans claim to hate their jobs, and some of them are surely smart enough to know why, but they don't know what to do with themselves without those jobs.

The California dream is not based on "country-club values," as Loud suggests. Rather, the dream is simply a bold attempt to turn the old ethic upside down, to put the priority of private time before the necessity of a job. The old phrase "working for a living" is close to what the dream is about. "Working for a life" might be still more accurate. The Western dream does indeed begin from the middle, not from the bottom, with an assumption of survival. Assuming survival, it says that people are entitled to pleasure themselves and that California has most of the pleasurable resources within daily driving range. It says you don't have to work fifty weeks for two weeks of pleasure.

A minority of Americans are able to enjoy that dream during waking hours. Those are the people who don't see sunshine as a secret sin, who don't share Bill Loud's bigotry about bare feet being debauched, who literally work to buy time, free time. Many airline pilots, however politically conservative, are personally liberated to liking leisure. Many University of California professors see no shameful paradox in wanting to teach where the surf is up and galoshes are never necessary. My friend Bill Glasgow, a senior editor at *Psychology Today,* has almost made a career out of cultivating garden time through desk time. The difference between Glasgow and other self-proclaimed gardeners is his California set of priorities. Glasgow is easily interrupted at the office. He does not insulate himself on the job. He does not trade on his title, aspire to new titles, or define himself by his editorship. He considers himself an outdoor grower who has to perform indoor work as a means of sustaining the habit. When he is enjoying his habit, Glasgow is not so easily reached, interrupted, or distracted. The garden is what he lives for; the job is no more than the means to the end.

38

Only a minority of us Californians have learned how to accept the upside-down ethic and enjoy it. That's why so many of us cringe when East Coast friends make their annual visits and deliver their angry reports on California sloth. Most of us still have a two-week-vacation mentality, thinking that working year-round justifies doing what we think we want to do for a couple of weeks.

The really radical nature of the California dream is the refutation of the whole "busy" ethic as it grew in western Europe, was transplanted in New York, and worked its way to Illinois and Indiana. Even Westerners talk the game better than we play it. But we try.

I mentioned Bloomington, Indiana, earlier in this chapter, partly because a man named John Sweet lives there. I've never met him, but he once wrote a letter to the Los Angeles *Times* that simply and touchingly described what's wrong with dream analysis applied to California:

It is the most western state, which makes it the place of the last frontier. Millions of Americans would *like* to see it as a place of hope, of progress, of better things. It is, in short, the coat-rack on which we would like to hang our dreams.

But we can't. California like every other cotton picking state in the nation of course has problems. But unlike other states, we feel it "shouldn't" have problems. We are sorry to find out that it does and so we jump up and down and beat on our highchairs with our spoons making angry little cries. The irrational charge is that YOU HAVE LET US DOWN.

A second reason for our displeasure with you is more important. As has been said so many times, California may be the wave of the future. It is what we are slowly becoming, all 49 of the rest of us. And we are terribly uncertain about that future and so we come out there and smell and nibble about and get more and more uneasy. We blame you for not being a better future, for not being perfect. As a matter of fact for the first time in our history, we have no real comfort or certainty about tomorrow. We just don't know where we are going or what we are going to be. And this is brand new. And nervous making.

And so my sunny California pards, cool it. We love you. Really we do. When we knock you we simply knock some things in ourselves we'd like to disappear—but it's going to take a while. We'd all like to have a better world. I am sure you join us there.

I like Sweet. He is more generous than the people we left behind in the mother countries of Massachusetts, New York, and New Jersey. But I also think he's wrong, from a California perspective, and I'd like to write back:

Dear John Sweet:
I understand why the rest of America would like to use California as a place to put its aspirations. We are young as well as western out here. I've often said we are the runaway children of a relatively young country, the first generation of

40

home-grown refugees spawned by the United States.

Good parents always hope for the best for their children. All parents tend to assign their own unrealized or imperfect successes to their children. I agree with you when you say that California, according to its parents, shouldn't have problems. But you are not the ones in high-chairs banging spoons and bawling. We are. Our optimism is selfish, personal, and private.

We don't want to be the wave of the future. Simple as that. Every time you or some other well-intentioned relative gives us that burden, we squirm like hell. California wants to be itself. Or, more honestly, California only wants to be it-selves, which may be ungrammatical but is closer to the multiple sorts of individualism practiced here.

If you can accept the idea of the West being full of American defectors, then you can also realize the chasm between what you want for us —or from us—and what we are trying to do for ourselves. The whole business of assigning the future to California was started by outsiders. Alexis de Tocqueville, the nineteenth-century French savant, dumped a similar burden on the United States. He came over to the brash new nation and decided it was where the future lived for everybody else. He liked democracy. He admired social experimentation. And I think he enjoyed surprising his contemporary countrymen by suggesting there was more to America than impudence and inelegance. The United States liked what de Tocqueville saw because the United States were still immature enough to want parental approval from Europe. The United States were also still obsessed with notions of manifest destiny, with arrogance about American ingenuity, with theological imperatives on the theme of representing God's will in God's odd world.

Californians know better. First, we are not a particularly pious society, despite our saved believers. The idea that any group can act out the will of God, if there is a God, sounds much too self-aggrandizing. And also too difficult. Second, we have few illusions about our supposed superior ingenuity or ability. Third, manifest destiny is another missionary concept, and few missionaries move among us. Finally, parental approval from the East would be all right if it weren't delivered with strings attached.

But the strings are always there. Californians are continually expected to be people they aren't. That's why Californians ran away in the first place. They didn't want to do the chores assigned. They are self-centered, self-serving, self-actuating, selfish individuals.

Can you accept that, John Sweet, without hating the kids who moved west from Eigenmann Avenue in Bloomington? Can you realize that the last thing a runaway wants is a new mandate from the place he left? Can you embrace the idea that mandates were what made those kids run in the first place?

If you can manage all those mental gymnas-

tics, then you won't have any trouble understanding why the California dream is to be rid of
future assignments.

I grant it's possible, for better or worse, that
California will be the model for tomorrow even if
California doesn't want to be. Long-haired kids
didn't want their elders to copy them, either.
Maybe all those self-absorbed characteristics of
Californians will be adopted by older cultures in
the country. But that will be a case of the adults
aping the children again, unasked and uninvited.

I find one aspect of all this extremely fascinating. The people who live with the most yester-
days are the ones most absorbed with tomorrows.
Californians, who have the least amount of past,
are less concerned with future. The West is a
present-tense phenomenon. When you write "We
just don't know where we are going or what we
are going to be," I think you speak for all Americans. But part of the pleasure of California has
been the breathing room and the freedom space to
avoid deciding what it wants to be when it grows
up.

California can tolerate all kinds of paradoxes
because it has no orthodoxy. It can live with
political extremes, sexual extravagances, mys-
tical excesses, and a kind of classlessness precisely because it has refused to decide what it
wants to be when it grows up. If California ever
does have certainty about tomorrow, then it won't
be so tolerant of all the peculiar creatures it
shelters today. We still have the luxury of in-
decision out here, like the perpetual college

student who refuses to pick a major because any major will determine what he or she does for the rest of his or her life.

That's also why most of us are not nationalists. We're not even statists, because there's no easy way to be a booster of something so ill-defined. When you write about everyone wanting a better world, I can't disagree with the aspiration. But California is still working on what a good world might be, right now.

So thanks, John, for all your conciliating words, but don't expect Californians to talk much about tomorrows, your tomorrows or theirs. Best to you and to Bloomington.

And if I were writing to Bill Loud, I think I'd try to explain another reason why Californians cringe at criticism. We really do want to be loved. Alas, we care what other people think. Part of the dream is wanting to be a star—and a star expects reviews. Wanting to be left alone and also wanting to star are not contradictory; that's exactly what the unlisted person of the previous chapter wants.

The show-biz background of Southern California continues to have a profound influence on all the people who live here. California is unplanned and uncohesive because all the players are worried about their own careers. The bottomless dancer wants her bottom to be admired, but she doesn't much care whether the critic likes the nightclub. California individual performers want to be loved, but they are less interested in what the visitor says about the state.

The love we want is mostly for particular performances. Later I'll try to explain our lack of loyalty to place, but it seems important here to emphasize how Californians take criticism. They take it personally.

A San Franciscan, for instance, has no anguish when an old friend from Connecticut comes west and talks about the yahoos and yo-yos who live in Los Angeles. He might not even be offended if the Connecticut Yankee made disparaging remarks about how lousily the San Francisco Giants play baseball, or how the new high-rises have made a blob out of Nob Hill, or how the local newspapers monger more gossip than information. If he is not offended by any of the above, it is because he has no intimate connection with his local ballclub, the overdevelopment of Nob Hill, or the news media. But let us assume our hypothetical San Franciscan is in the food business. Then he will accept no criticism suggesting San Francisco restaurants have deteriorated, implying Napa Valley wines are not comparable to France's, hinting sourdough bread is without nutritional value. The whole city is only the nightclub where he does his bottomless dance. But aspersions cast against his closest associations are arrows in his own exposed behind.

Each Californian is contantly rehearsing his or her act. Each Californian is constantly auditioning that act for neighbors, tourists, and critics. Each of us is insecure enough to believe that he or she is only as good as his or her last review. The California dream, in fact, involves an eternal personal rehearsal for a production that never quite opens.

The production never closes, either, which is the optimistic way to look at perpetual student-performers.

When Julia Newman left Los Angeles in 1974, her friend Rosemary Howard wrote:

"I loved the part in your letter about the possibility of your return to the East Coast because we've all been mourning you since you left. Do *not*, *NOT* think that returning would be a failing, a giving up. Like everything else in life, it's not the *what*, it's the *why*, the personal *why* that counts—and assembling your life to get the most things possible sounds like a great victory to me."

Julia Newman, about to return to New York after a couple of years in California, reacted to her friend's obvious supportiveness:

"Rosemary is one of the dearest people in my life, and she had, in her concern for me, picked up from my conversation—actually probably projected into it—something I wasn't feeling: defeat. The time here will have been a time of transition for me, of building the bridge from one part of my life to the next, from one career to another. I've gained access to capabilities that I hardly dared guess I possessed. I hadn't ever written anything but letters and school papers before I came here. Somehow, here, I found permission that I couldn't grant myself in New York, the permission to write."

Newman's ping-ponging between coasts illustrates the difference between the ends of America. She was a successful maker of television commercials during her New York incarnation. She had more pride in her process than in her product—a fairly typical attitude in the advertising trade. Julia Newman moved west to attempt a couple of improvements in her life. If she was going to make commercials anyway, she might as well make them in a warmer location. And if she was going to try her hand at other crafts, then she might as well clean out some of the drawers and debris attached to living in New York.

She learned at least two lessons in Los Angeles. One is the economic fact of life we will consider later at some length: Most of the American money grows in the East. Some money is exported to the West, but cash is the one green crop best cultivated in New York, along the banks of the financial community. That meant Julia's commercial work essentially originated in New York, even though she was a California resident, even though some of the sponsors did their business on the West Coast. The plotting funding and hiring was still a function of Madison Avenue. The other lesson had to do with her wanting to work in print as well as in film. There were publishing outfits in Los Angeles that would be receptive to her work. You can get a reading in the West. Anybody can. Even publishers are optimists out here, expecting the best. Julia Newman managed to produce a quite competent exposé on a couple of businesses that were using the specter of universal starvation to sell processed, storable foodstuffs. And she went on to do a good piece on what to do with an automotive lemon shipped from Detroit to Los Angeles. *Coast Magazine,* a monthly, bought both articles and presented them with attractive art direction. But *Coast Magazine,* not so unlike Julia Newman, is itself a relatively young upstart. *Coast* cannot afford to pay more than a couple of hundred dollars for a piece that may take three or four weeks to research and write. Lesson two was that the West has an appetite for what you do, but the West can't necessarily support you at it. California is receptive, much more so than the East. Your act has a chance to audition, and you may even find a stage. The trouble is, playing the provinces does not pay.

So Julia Newman took her lessons, packed them up, and went back where the money is. She's not defeated, because she's now confident about being able to do more than her previous sponsors were willing to buy. In the East, she had picked her major and she was expected to stay with her choice. In the West, she developed her own curriculum and was allowed to chase her own curiosities. Maybe Julia Newman has the best of both worlds back in New York. My guess is that she hitched a piece of the California dream to her own drives and came away with a vehicle that will one day sustain her on either coast.

I've been trying to avoid the cliché "doing your own thing" for several thousand words now. But, alas and dammit, the phrase is appropriate to this discussion. California is where your own thing may be the only thing you can do. And that's where the risk is, along with the self-gratification.

One aspect of this egocentric approach to a place is unhappy and unsettling. Borrowing another slogan from the teen-agers, millions of Californians claim they can't relate to other people because they don't yet know themselves—or they can't participate in community activity until they get their shit together. I hear that excuse in a variety of phrases in a variety of socio-economic groups in a variety of age groups. Californians, with all their sense of permission, are not so good in a social context. They refuse to believe that the only way to get one's shit together is with other people who are trying to make order out of waste.

I blame Lana Turner, or the myth of Lana Turner, for much of the trouble. The old story about the pretty girl sitting at Schwab's in a vanilla sweater is a dangerous segment of the California dream, extending beyond show business to much of the population.

The key is that the girl was waiting to be discovered, sitting passively in front of soda jerks. No New Yorker expects such things. An Easterner expects to be ordered to move on to make room for paying customers, expects to be pushed, elbowed, harried, and even molested. But Californians cling to the idea that a person can find herself or himself in isolation and then wait for discovery.

That's the part of the dream I think Bill Loud was really upset about, about young people who don't take their lives in their own hands but instead imagine there are agents around every corner looking for the shit they have put together.

The interesting footnote to the Loud saga is that two thirds of the former family moved to New York after the rupture. Only Bill Loud and one of his sons stayed West. Pat Loud and four offspring moved to Manhattan. Jon Nordheimer, in the same *New York Times* article, quoted Pat on her relocation: "New York is a big exciting place . . . where everything happens, filled with people with heavy drives, scratching their way up. And now we are all unabashedly trying to cash in on our instant fame. If it hadn't been for the series we'd probably still be in the slow, boring ambience of Santa Barbara."

"Boring" is a big word among dreamers who've lost their illusions. "Boring" was the word used by so many Irvine, California, teen-agers who found dope dealing preferable to the prescribed life in a planned community. We'll meet them in later pages. Being bored is a self-inflicted state, usually possible only in a place where there are freedoms and where extraordinary demands are not placed on the individual. Warm weather and the time to make personal decisions cannot be boring. Only an inability to enjoy that time makes Jack a bored boy. The people who make the California dream come true and then live it out happily are the people who honestly, unashamedly like to play. The pople who continue to thrive on assigned work, on other people's expectations, on the security of knowing one's place in a place should stay East.

We have warped our sense of time out here to suit our sense of place. We make our own hours, which the good commuters of Grand Central may find difficult to understand.

-IV-

Out of Time, Out of Bounds

The California calendar and the California clock are creations of the dream, unlike the standard time of the East Coast.

The West is wide open, at least commercially, and that all-days, all-hours salesmanship caters to a different kind of crowd. Optimism allows the sellers to keep businesses operating non-stop. And a sense of convenience—that the world was created for their comfort —allows buyers to expect that everything is available whenever the whim for anything happens to arise.

The all-night massage parlors are no surprise, because the urge to be rubbed is one of those whims born of drink or loneliness or caprice.

But California has more mundane attractions working around the clock—markets, for instance. The Hollywood Ranch Market on Vine Street has become something of a legend, where winos and millionaires can meet and squeeze grapefruit at four in the morning. The Ranch Market was once something of a curiosity, even in California. Now there are many markets that offer nourishment on a twenty-four-hour basis.

One of my favorites is Boys', in Encino. Encino is a well-to-do suburb of Los Angeles, comparable to Scarsdale, Bryn Mawr, and Framingham in terms of average annual income. The Boys' Market opened in the sixties as Piggly Wiggly Continental, one of the oddest ventures in an odd state. Piggly Wiggly was an old national chain, with strong links in agricultural Middle America. The Continental was added to the Encino branch in an effort to curl a little class into the Piggly Wiggly tail. It was a beautiful supermarket indeed, as supermarkets go: fresh-fish section, delicatessen area with prepared hot foods available for catered dinners, mammoth produce bins with exotic fruits from the Pacific Islands, a bakery, and a liquor store with a handsome selection of California wines. I used to take tourists there, because it was the most opulent attraction in the San Fernando Valley.

But poor old Piggly Wiggly could not live comfortably in such a fancy neighborhood. Boys' came in several years later, with an advance reputation for meeting upper-middle needs. Now Boys' Encino store, the former Continental, is open all the time. And the remarkable experience is finding people from a sleepy suburb in the place at five A.M.

I used to think World War II had something to do with grocers going all the way. Swing shifts in the old aircraft plants put shoppers on peculiar schedules; they brought home the bacon when they could.

But there are probably more twenty-four-hour operations now than there ever were when we were remembering Pearl Harbor. Californians, especially Southern Californians, merely like to set their own schedules. Just as the automobile spoiled them in terms of commuting according to personal schedule instead of train schedule, it also gave them an eccentric sense of errand running, in which the track must adjust to the runner.

We have all-night laundromats, too. Some of them attract chess players who sit for hours while their clothes are being agitated. Some of them are where actors hang out and memorize their lines during the wash cycle. Some of them are social halls for single swingers—what better place to compare tastes and fashions than where everyone's underwear is part of the routine?

We have all-night private eyes, an opportunity Raymond Chandler or Ross MacDonald would applaud. The Hargrave Secret Service, for example, advertises: "Offices open day and night, Sundays and holidays . . . Security Guards for all occasions." The Scientific Investigation Agency provides the same eternal vigilance after asking: "Spouse unfaithful? Activity reports for your peace of mind." Intercept Inc. is another, boasting "qualified experts with a progressive approach to age old problems."

Among the four Yellow Pages in Los Angeles occupied by private eyes, more than one dozen claim to do it round-the-clock. One never knows when dark suspicion will cross the mind of a California client.

We used to have all-night public dumps, where you could pay your money and dispose of anything you didn't want to haul—or were afraid to haul—by daylight. They seem to have disappeared, possibly a casualty of the energy crisis. Or maybe dumpers became worried about their own safety in doing trash disposal by night.

We still have a few all-night florists, in case love or sympathy strikes before dawn.

And we have more all-night restaurants than the rest of the English-speaking world. In California, one can eat, shop, spy, launder, and send flowers at any time. A Chevrolet agency near Long Beach used to sell cars around the clock, but the television ads no longer brag about such eternal dealing.

Strangely enough, the bars are not allowed to stay open as late as they do in New York. California entertains no public drinking after two A.M.—a small hardship more than made up for by the availability of booze at all other times.

The seven-day week is a staple of the retail liquor business. And liquor may be bought in supermarkets, department stores, and drugstores as well as plain old liquor stores. The Lord may have rested on Sunday, but Californians use Sundays to go about their serious business of chasing pleasure. I know one Christian woman who had the gall the offer her home for sale on Easter Sunday; it sold within forty-five minutes, at her divine asking price.

Sunday in the West is not only big for selling houses, it's also time for merchandising furniture and food, appliances and automobiles, clothes and cosmetics, books and bric-a-brac. In increasing numbers, department stores are staying open on the Sabbath. As designer Jeffrey Lindsay once said, the suburban shopping center has become the plaza–cathedral–sidewalk café of modern America, especially western

America. People not only visit the shopping center to satisfy their materialistic appetites, they also go to meet friends, dine out, ice skate, see live entertainers, and ogle the human comedy.

Sunday in California has also become the day for swap meets, garage sales, and horse races. The old Pennsylvania blue laws were never honored in the West, but as the West expands its capacities for business and pleasure, Sunday has become the most profitable day of the week for getting and spending and gambling.

Pagan? Partly. Also pious. California retains its famous religious fervor, and has hitched some of it to the automobile. The Garden Grove Community Church, in conservative Orange County, was the nation's first major drive-in chapel. A growing congregation without a house of worship to call home rented a drive-in movie theater during the fifties for its regular services. The arrangement made excellent economic sense: The theater owners couldn't show films in the daytime, and the churchgoers didn't have to have devotions at night. But by the time the congregation could afford to build its own facility, the drive-in had become a hit and a habit for other reasons.

Mothers and fathers of small children discovered they could take their kids to church without worrying about offending other adults as long as the kids could stay in a car. The children could attend to the faith, and their parents saved the baby-sitting fee. Old people learned how churchgoing in an automobile saved steps. And the seats of the family sedan were much softer than unupholstered pews. Sick people were happy to have drive-in services for similar reasons.

So, when the collection plates had been filled from car windows for a few years and the funds for a real church were available, the Garden Grovers opted for a devotional drive-in they could call their own. The late Richard Neutra, one of California's pioneer modern architects, was hired to design a dual facility, with indoor and outdoor worship areas. Neutra's solution was a kind of pie-shaped project, with the minister standing on a platform at the center of the pie and the congregation fanned out in adjoining indoor-outdoor segments. The result pleased the parishioners, and it also satisfied most critics of design.

Contrary to myth, Californians spend more time at home on weekends than do their Eastern aunts and uncles.

I lived in Philadelphia for the better part of a bad year in 1961, in a series of hotel rooms. At the twilight of every Friday I watched an incredible exodus as urban Pennsylvanians took trains, cars, and airplanes out of their city for a couple of days of supposed peace in the country. Philadelphia people didn't want to be in Philadelphia once the work was done. The city was payday, but it was no place to be.

Washington, D.C., has a similar repulsion for the people who work there. So does New York. The escape instinct is extraordinary in the East. The desire for a second home, where weekends will be bearable, is stronger on the Atlantic than the Pacific. Even now, when I visit the East Coast, I can find my friends between Monday and Friday but lose track of them if I happen to arrive on Saturday.

I think East Coast residents secretly hate their homes.

Home, for them, seems to be an extension of job, of all the chores and pains they must accept in order to buy forty-eight hours of freedom every weekend plus a few weeks of holiday each summer. In the East, home is a function of work, often chosen on the basis of train schedule or distance to the subway. Home is the logistical base where one draws food and supplies for the next day's warfare; it's not the place one wants to be in peacetime.

The opposite is generally true in California, where the premium is on pleasure and the job is second priority.

Western folklore is full of stories about the astonishing distances between the person's job and his or her house. The man who lives in Sausalito and works in San Mateo. The woman who commutes between Laguna and Los Angeles. The person on Point Loma who keeps shop above La Jolla. Almost every book about California in the last decade included the tale of the family that lived, full time, in its vehicle.

The story was first told by Willian Bronson in *Cry California,* the usually sober quarterly sponsored by California Tomorrow, a non-profit organization committed to planning and conservation. When Bronson told it, campers and other recreation vehicles were just beginning to hit the highways. The idea of a family rolling around the California freeway system forever—sleeping in the vehicle near off-ramps, spending the day in a constant pickup and delivery of various members—was both outrageous and believable.

It was outrageous in the mid-sixties because most Americans—even most Californians—couldn't accept the notion of a house in perpetual motion. It was

57

believable, even then, because Californians were already famous for the distances they were willing to accept in order to be their own dispatchers. Several newspapers and broadcast outlets picked up Bronson's story as a news item, only to learn that it was fantasy, pure fantasy based on future probability.

The fantasy came true, of course, before the decade was done. Young Californians became the market for the van, a hybrid vehicle that was part bus, part truck, part bedroom, and part car. Young Californians liked to live in the vans that saved on rent, kept fixed possessions to a minimum, and offered the illusion of freedom. Vans became true mobile homes, unlike the so-called mobile homes anchored in trailer parks. The young people made a prophet out of Bronson. They also managed to find support from the less mobile society, moving in on friends and relatives for such refinements as showers, commodes, and clothes washers. I'm not sure the van people consider themselves parasites in any way, but they are a kind of nomad, adrift partly through the kindness of non-drifters.

In another way, the van people are the apotheosis of the California dream as it affects clocks and calendars. They've made their homes their whole lives, and all other chores, appointments, errands have been made subordinate to the way they roll around. Destinations are much less important than the going. If the going is good, then the other details can be attended to.

Less mobile Californians also tend to love their homes, which is why they accept herculean distances for daily drives to work. Home is a vacation itself. And that's why the sprawl has been sustained so long.

58

I have a friend who moved toward Los Angeles from a faraway suburb because of the energy crisis of 1974, because she had never tried working within walking range, because she wanted to test herself in a socio-economic hodgepodge.

Two weeks after beginning the big experiment, she discovered she missed her freeway. In the past she never had claimed to love her freeway. In fact, she had lived with it as a necessary nuisance—never taken for good; just for granted. When she lived forty driving miles from the offce, the driving time could be as long as one hundred ten minutes during jam-up hours. She sometimes used the freeway time to consider what life might be like if one shrank the space between the personal and professional, if one could be at one with the city. Out of bed and into work without dependence on a machine. No SigAlerts (California's funny name for traffic warnings) could stop her if she made the move. No more air-conditioned insulation from the sights, smells, sounds of the city. If she moved within walking distance of the job, the town would be at her feet, at human scale.

What she forgot during such fantasizing was the way she used freeway time, even traffic jam-up time. That was when she did all her private planning and self-sorting and California daydreaming. The encapsulation all the urban critics criticize, the steely insulation of West Coast commuting, was her secret refuge from any place and everybody. She began to think that maybe, after all, being nowhere is the only "where" in which to be free—an echo of the van people, who don't much value destinations.

The freeways are our modern open spaces,

however ugly the metaphor may first appear. Because they encapsulate the individual, they leave all room and time for contemplation. They are psychological open spaces, even if set in concrete and filled with signs. They are the great punctuation marks between work and home which keep the house free of business matters. When the East Coast commuter covers large distances, he or she usually has to carry a newspaper or a briefcase full of work to hide behind in order to approach such freedom. Those barriers—the paper or the homework—are themselves distractions from any pure dreaming.

The woman who pulled in her roots to be near work now resents her work more than she ever did in the old days when she maintained so much distance between office and home. She misses her freeway because she misses herself. Now there's only family time and colleague time. The Californian wants more from the clock: selfish time. The freeway was her excuse for being selfish, although she never knew it until she came to town. The freeway was her yoga exercise, her means of meditation.

My friend, in moving, was living more like a New Yorker. Home was not simply closer to the office; it became connected with the office. And part of her resentment came from the realization that she had compromised her life for the sake of convenience to her job. That's what East Coast people, still with the old ethic in their skulls, do all the time. California people try to suit themselves first and then worry about work that will be convenient.

One way to appreciate how New Yorkers attach home and office, thereby creating a need to escape from both, is to realize the non-availability of restaurants on Sunday evenings. In New York, a majority of the good dining rooms are closed, because the residents have fled town. Only the hotels, catering to tourists and conventioneers, are all open for customers. In San Francisco, almost the opposite is true. Sunday is a big night for the locals, because the locals have stayed home to have their weekend pleasures. New York and San Francisco are supposed to have several similarities: large pedestrian populations; concentrated, comprehensible downtown areas; sophisticated citizenries that appreciate the fine arts, the performing arts, and fancy foreign cooking. But San Franciscans tend to think of their city as their pleasure, not their penance. They stick around to play around. The office is something that happens to be there. Home is something to enjoy.

A few other aspects of Pacific time are worth a few moments.

One is the appointment, business or pleasure, for which Westerners are invariably late. Disliking imposed schedules, they do not honor them well at all. The acceptable slippage for a social dinner party is forty-five minutes in California. Thirty minutes is about average, the half-hour-tardy couple is generally preferred to the people who arrive on time.

One of my residual East Coast fetishes is punctuality. When I am punctual, which is almost all the time, I am embarrassing. When I am punctual for dinner, my host and hostess are still dressing in some back room. Rarely have they been ready for me in fifteen years of California residence. When I am punctual for a working appointment, I am one up on the other party.

He or she is the one who has to arrive on the jog, feigning being out of breath and explaining that there was an awesome tieup on the Santa Monica Freeway. I rather enjoy being apologized to.

The amusement industry, I'm convinced, is part of the California heritage for delay. Movies were always made by waiting—waiting for equipment to work, waiting for the sun to strike a proper posture over the pass, waiting for a missing prop to be delivered. Movie stars learned, by waiting experience, how to avoid being mussed or fussed by delays. What the stars learned was how to cause their own delays. The individual artist was able to triumph over the fumbling crew and the philistine company. Being prompt almost became a symbol of insecurity in Hollywood. The person who knew his or her own worth knew the rest of the world would wait. The person who was worried about his or her place under the lights was the one who had to be there on time.

In New York and Boston, tardiness is an insult. In Los Angeles and San Francisco, tardiness is to be tolerated, even welcomed. In New York and Boston, business rules the clock: time is indeed money. In Los Angeles and San Francisco, the clock is set by more eccentric standards; time is twisted by the mutual needs of the people sharing it.

As people have been saying for a century, the pace is different in California. New Yorkers run in tunnels; Californians crawl in pools. But the wealthy Californians I know expend no less energy than Easterners; they simply believe it's bad form to show it.

The individual is more important in the West than whatever time-motion clock he is supposed to punch. Social scientists used to claim climate as a force in moving people on their appointed rounds. Human beings who lived in harsh weather were supposed to move faster, if only to get in out of the cold or snow or rain. Creatures who lived in more tropical zones were supposed to be slowed by the sunshine. Cold was rousing. Heat was drowsing. But Americans have so thoroughly controlled their climates by now that it hardly matters much whether someone works in the chill of Providence or the warmth of Palo Alto.

Now California time, with its built-in delays, seems to be a statement that the individual is more important than any system served. The teen-agers who refuse to wear watches have carried that peculiar asocial custom to its maximum timelessness; they learned it on the Coast, where so many other mores of the young were born.

Another upside-down sense of urgency was probably created by the movie business. The telephone call is the most immediate weapon of communication in California for business purposes. The letter, complete with explanation, usually comes next. The least critical communiqué is usually the telegram. In the East, a wire was always associated with crisis or congratulation; it was considered the surest quick way of attracting somebody else's attention in a time of need. In California, a wire is often an invitation to an entertainment opening or a charity luncheon or a plain old cocktail party thrown for public relations purposes.

What happened in the West was the degrading of the telegram. Some smart show-biz agents long ago decided to use wires as a way of pretending importance. Wires cost money. They come in their own unique wrapping. They have a history of celebrating joy and documenting tragedy. They are relatively dependable. So publicists adopted telegrams as a means of underlining the unimportant, as a way to trick people into reading material that otherwise might be thrown away. It worked for a while. But now the wire is readily recognized in Hollywood as carrying more puffery than urgency.

Visitors from the East are understandably confused by such chicanery. The telegram retains some of its traditional shock value in New York and some of its political value in Washington, where citizen responses to government issues are weighed, if not studied. The Eastern priority would still put the telegram on top of the pile, the letter next, and the phone call last. East Coast business people have a better understanding of the telephone as an instrument of tyranny; why should a busy person answer up without a previous appointment or prior explanation?

The telephone continues to work strange wonders in the West because busy people have that sense of being available for business I described earlier, and because they have a false feeling that conversation is more direct than mail and more human than telegram. Besides, the movie business also taught several generations of impressionable people to be afraid of putting things to paper. The entertainment industry tried to use the handshake rather than the contract in the old days. It seemed warmer. It also allowed for weaseling without penalty. Now the lawyers so dominate the amusements that deals are as long and complicated as peace treaties. The usual practice is for the principals to make their arrangements verbally before committing them to the expensive job of written demands from warring counselors.

The telephone for urgency suits a state that dresses more easily, attends dates more casually, and sets its calendars more tardily for its own convenience. Californians are not unreliable. They are only concerned with keeping all the options open all the time.

I admit that I've still lessons to learn before completing my West Coast conversion. Not only is the old promptness obsession still in my gut, the freeway options are still not open to me. When I drive, I have to have a destination in mind. And the destination prevents me from the dreaming and nosepicking enjoyed in adjacent lanes. Californians are so self-contained that they really do pick their noses on the freeways, as if nobody were looking. I'm usually too concerned with some deadline somewhere to let myself go while behind the wheel, to enjoy the insularity.

Now that I think about it, I'm amazed that the California booms brought so much wealth to a state that went off standard time so long ago. I suppose weather made us rich as well as restless. We are the second wealthiest place in the country. But that still leaves us way behind number one, as readers at either pole will soon appreciate.

-V-

The Hangar Hangup and Other Instabilities

Two discoveries, gold and oil, made California what it is today.

Two inventions, the airplane and the motion picture, laid the basis for later booms.

All four industries attracted the more speculative spirits of America. The gold rush up north established San Francisco as the financial capital of the West Coast. The oil gush down south dappled the hills with drill rigs.

All four industries turned out to be unstable. Gold ran out, and the Mother Lode country around Sacramento gave the world some new ghost towns. Oil fields shifted as one part of Southern California after another was drilled and then drained, leaving scars along the landscape and pushing exploration out to offshore sites at Santa Barbara and Long Beach. Movies created Hollywood, but then the making of movies moved all over the world; Hollywood turned to television and the music business for survival. Aviation grew up to become aerospace, subject to changes in defense policy, national posture, and porkbarrel politics.

Critics of California architecture never gave enough credit—or blame—to oil, movies, and aerospace as essentially ugly industries. Derricks and drill rigs can at best be camouflaged to look like office buildings. Oil operations are noisy, smelly, and sticky. Airplanes were built in hangars which looked like factories. Movies were built in sound stages which looked like hangars.

Even today, Burbank Studios and Lockheed Burbank are remarkably similar facilities. Howard Hughes must have felt equally at home in his aircraft plant and his old RKO movie factory.

San Francisco began with beautiful topography and the banking business, meaning San Francisco was immediately recognizable as a city to people whose perspective came from Europe or the East Coast.

Los Angeles's famous sprawl grew logically from three businesses that splattered horizontally across the land: oil, aviation, and film. Architectural historians David Gebhard and Robert Winter wrote that look-at-me materialism became the bedrock for Southern California building: "Since it has been the individual and his material wants which have dominated the scene, it has naturally been the individual house, more than any other form of building, which has occupied the attention of architects and clients."

Partly true. But the individual house was the only practical way for wealthy Southern Californians to flaunt their egos. The amusement business and the aviation business did not lend themselves to splendid urban design. And we love our houses as distinct from our offices.

For decades Los Angeles and San Diego were branch-office towns. Few corporate headquarters came to Southern California, and so the office buildings that occupied the downtowns were ventures in speculative real estate rather than monuments to mammoth firms.

The old jokes about Los Angeles being so many suburbs in search of a city were East Coast jokes, because East Coast people had never seen a metropolis made out of a hangar mentality.

The individual residences studied by Gebhard and Winter are all over the Southern California map, all over the 460 square miles that locate Los Angeles alone. There are fancy houses in Pasadena, San Marino, Beverly Hills, Encino, Bel-Air, Pacific Palisades, and Palos Verdes, to place-drop only a few. There are historically distinguished contributions by Frank Lloyd Wright, R. M. Schindler, Richard Neutra, and the Greene brothers. There are more rich neighborhoods within twenty miles of downtown Los Angeles than around other major American cities.

The houses in those rich neighborhoods change owners more often than in other major American cities. The people of California move once every three years, on the average. Some of the movement is merely a symptom of West Coast mobility, a going through the motions that will be considered later. Some of the movement is an immediate reflection of instability. Layoffs in aerospace and failures in film produce massive residential shifts.

The richest and most permanent residents of Beverly Hills and Bel-Air are the professional people who service instability: doctors and lawyers. Movie stars come and go, making tourist maps of celebrity mansions obsolete each season. But the attorneys who minister to movie stars are not subject to flops and fads. The doctors who take care of the most-cared-for bodies on earth earn their six-figure incomes no matter who has the number-one hit record or who made the last cover of *Time*. The psychiatrists, psychologists, and other mental healthists are almost an elite unto themselves; Beverly Hills has more brain practitioners per capita than any city in the United States—a spectacular case of mind over matter. The treatment of instability breeds its own stability. The doctors and lawyers, not the stars who portray rulers and Indian chiefs, are the people who live longest in the houses with the Grecian pools and the Italian cypress trees and the two-Mercedes carports.

California has a calamity climate, as unstable as its commerce, regardless of how tediously the sun seems to shine down south. In addition to earthquakes, the state is famous for fires and floods. When Bel-Air burned to a fraction of its former self in the early sixties, Zsa Zsa Gabor stood in the ruins of her former residence and claimed such tragedies shouldn't happen in such nice neighborhoods. But they do, and frequently. Carl Reiner said when it rains in New York people get wet; when it rains in Los Angeles people get killed. That's hardly hyperbole; Southern California drains poorly, its freeways turn slick at the first rains because of accumulated oil, its slippery geology is not water-repellent. Fire in the highly flammable Southern California chaparral usually leads to flood when new rain rolls down bare hillsides. And flood is often followed by landslide as rain continues and seeps into the shale below the surface.

Climate is more than weather, however, and weather was what brought both the invention of flight and the invention of films to California. The aviation people wanted to manufacture wings where there was a reasonable probability of open sky. And the movie pioneers wanted to make film where there was the least chance of being dripped on or snowed over during the great chase.

Terry Ramsaye's history of the movie business, *A Million and One Nights,* starts at such places as Philadelphia, Brooklyn, and the Edison lab in Newark. Not until 1907, with the arrival of a director named Francis Boggs, did the movie people discover Los Angeles. A company named New York Motion Picture made the move soon after, seduced by the promise of sunshine and scared by a real brawl between its actors and professional gangsters during filmmaking on Long Island. D. W. Griffith of Biograph came to California in 1910 and set up shop in a vacant lot. When Griffith couldn't find enough people locally to play in his West Coast productions, the call went out for unemployed Broadway actors, and so began the migration of performers from the legitimate stages of New York to the movie lots of Los Angeles. So also began the eternal controversy over the West as the center of artifice and the East as the center of art. Many actors were ashamed to have to leave the stage to appear in something as slapdash and ephemeral as the early motion pictures. Movies couldn't talk yet, but casts could complain.

Artists tended to be night people, and movies were strictly a daytime trade. The very sunshine that shifted a new industry was alien to its hired hands.

Some of the people who came to play in California saw it as a sinful act from the start. The writers and directors and leading players who followed them often felt the same taint of sun. Working with the dawn was unnatural. Going west was an adventure, but only a traitor would make it a career.

In contrast, technologists found the going good. When the airplane industry flourished on the West Coast during World War II, thousands of engineers and technicians flew to Douglas, Lockheed, Convair, North American, and Boeing factories from Seattle to San Diego.

They and their families stayed on after the war. They were joined by servicemen who had passed through California on their way to the battles of the Pacific. Then came the think tankers, the elites of technology and philosophy, who included systems analysts and scientists paid to ponder instead of produce. Rand Corporation set up its tank at Santa Monica and argued strategy for the U.S. Air Force from a bluff overlooking the ocean. Robert Hutchins took his Center for the Study of Democratic Institutions and put it among the tall trees of Montecito, just outside Santa Barbara. A visiting journalist of the late fifties saw the splendor of the Center and said he'd finally witnessed "the leisure of the theory class." Simon Ramo and Dean Wooldridge opened their own shop and raised technology's sights to the missile age.

Scientists and engineers saw no sin in sunshine. California universities found they could lure distinguished scholars with the promise of adequate pay, convenient consulting opportunities, and warm weather.

The postwar population boom was not the baby of the amusement business but the child of academics and aerospace workers and advanced theorists. They were the white collars, now open at the throat, who bought the tract houses, the outdoor barbecues, the backyard swimming pools, and the suburban sunshine styles.

The people who stayed east were the money manipulators and the media mongers. The people who moved west were the skilled laborers and the science manipulators—two classses of Americans that tended not to carry traditions or club memberships with them.

All the migrants might have lived happily ever after if they hadn't been so dependent on the federal government back east. The Korean War kept the airframe industry reasonably intact through the early fifties. Then the Russian launch of Sputnik in 1957 produced an aftershock in America, and the United States began its own rocket boom. John Kennedy committed the country to the moon in the early sixties, and components for the moon were to be built in California.

But custom-crafted missilry is not mass-produced aircraft. And peaceful space exploration doesn't require as many missiles as a weaponry program. Once America had built its ration of ballistic missiles and stored them underground or underwater, there was little need for new ones. Once Lyndon Johnson became President, there were political reasons for shifting some of America's aerospace contracts to the South and Southwest. Missiles were built in Houston, and California was left in a technological lurch, with a mammoth work force and not enough work. The industrial giants of aerospace looked for new stability in fields such as city planning, surface transportation systems, and deliveries of social services. Diversity has not come easy, and flexibility has not come fast; the state that hitched its prosperity to the tail of rockets has been scrambling for the last decade, laying off skilled technicians and engineers even before the Vietnam War had dragged to a ceasefire.

Meanwhile, the movie industry was being absorbed by conglomerates, huge holding companies with no sense of Hollywood and only a financial interest in what film can produce. One by one, the old moguls died: Louis B. Mayer, Harry Cohn, David Selznick, Sam Goldwyn. The moguls may not have been Beautiful People, but they had roots in California even while most movie business offices were in the East. The old studios turned into vacant lots again, and then into real-estate ventures. Twentieth Century–Fox was sold off to Alcoa and became Century City, a complex of commercial high-rises. MGM was sliced up into housing and other unmagical properties. The old Warner Brothers became Burbank Studios, with several firms huddled together, sharing a diminished need for sound stages. Universal managed to stabilize its acreage by making television shows, and by taking tourists on paying tours to see where movies used to be made.

California sunshine is no longer needed to make motion pictures, but the rest of the entertainment industry—especially pop music and television—has moved in to make work for craftspeople and performers.

The resident millionaires of amusement, aerospace, and oil rarely mix. Whenever an East Coast writer comes to Southern California looking for the local power structure, a power structure never appears. Los Angeles is not Pittsburgh and steel, not Hartford and insurance, not Washington and bureaucracy, not Boston and medicine.

The state of California doesn't lend itself to quick compression either. San Francisco has large banks and little kinship with cities south of the Tehachapi Mountains. Sacramento, the state capital, is farm country with a patch of government growing in its midst. Los Angeles, where the people live, is still considered the ugly upstart, conceived through an illegitimate affair between people and automobiles, spawning an unlovable bastard, smog.

Los Angeles is simply not comprehensible to some San Franciscans and most East Coast observers. The national center of gravity is bounded by Boston and Washington, with its heaviest pull in New York. But the farther one is from the center of gravity, the more fun one is likely to have from life with less pull, less pressure. Where the action is may also be where the routine is, leaving little room for the exquisite pleasures of random discovery and rich surprise. California would be wrecked if it tried to be another New York, and then the sun might as well never have risen on the western empire.

Living so well, we don't want to die. At least, we don't want to die without doing something about it.

Death has been a big business in California for decades. My first memory of the southern section of the Golden State was a mammoth billboard for a mortuary advertising FOREVERNESS, with a simple portrait of Moses in the background.

The largest local death servicer of them all, Forest Lawn, used to brag about undertaking every last ritual, "all in one place." In 1974 Forest Lawn turned to comedy, and one of the classic radio commercials of all time—even eternity, perhaps—is a man-in-the-street interview with a visitor from Detroit.

The announcer suggests that the Midwesterner has come to California because he's interested in burial services. No, protests, the tourist, "I came to live a little." The announcer says that's understandable if you're from Detroit, underlining the prejudice on both coasts toward the uninhabitable center. The announcer insists that the people of Detroit are concerned about how reasonable burial can be at Forest Lawn: less than six hundred dollars per body for nearly one third of the digs performed last year. No, repeats the tourist, claiming astonishment at arriving at a California depot for a terminal interview.

Easterners have consistently thought of California as a sick joke because of the blatant commercialization of death. The English couldn't agree more: Waugh's *Loved One* and Huxley's *After Many a Summer Dies the Swan* are classic consumer satires on California funeral retailing. As evidence that death copies art, tourists cite the various Forest Lawn mortuaries with their alabaster sculptures, copies of Old Masters, movie-set chapels, and recreated temples.

The visitors are amazed to discover that Forest Lawn also caters to life, offering facilities for weddings, anniversaries, and other commemorative celebrations of the human spirit.

The clue is there. Forest Lawn is a well joke, not a sick one. Forest Lawn and its FOREVERNESS competitors have converted death into a crazy sort of lifestyle. Advertising death, promoting burial plots with a view, bragging about coffins that are seepage-proof, the mortuaries of California have turned the undiscussable into another free enterprise, subject to everyday conversation. Mortuaries even advertise on bus-stop benches, thereby providing a temporary resting place for the human body in anticipation of permanent needs.

Sculptor Ed Kienholz has been obsessed with death and morality from a particularly California perspective. His room-size vignettes—*Living War Memorial, Barney's Beanery, The Wait*—are abrasive attempts to pull the shrouds off death and make it part of life. Forest Lawn simply does the same thing, with less profundity but more flash.

California can assimilate death because it concentrates on individual life and personal hedonism. The East Coast concentrates on corporate life; in such context, death is almost unthinkable, because it would be an admission that business was bad and early retirement had been ordered by a higher power. In California, sky diving and drag racing are a flouting of the death fear. In New York and Washington, deadbolt door locks are hard concessions to the death fear.

Death can only be a well joke where life is an amusement. The industrial society, centered in the East, has always allowed minimal time for amusement—those couple of weeks with pay and the privilege of wasting weekends in traffic jams between shore and mountains.

Economic futurists such as Robert Heilbroner and literary futurists such as Toffler are now telling us the industrial society is itself dying, strangling because of pollution, diminished resources, dehumanizing densities, and radical changes in human aspirations. We are supposed to be emerging into the post-industrial society, a vague place of peril and opportunity which might seem to suit the West Coast flair for disorganized individualism.

The reality of right now, however, can't be ignored. Politicians may mislead us when they kneel to California and label it the foremost state in body count and the second state in business. Second place is nowhere near New York, not even close to the East Coast in terms of industrial might.

A little hard data is appropriate. A 1970s *Fortune* directory of the five hundred largest industrial corporations in the United States can be read as a comparative index to the two coasts.

Not one of the top ten firms of the seventies lives in California, whereas seven of the top ten headquarter in New York. Only one of the top twenty, Standard Oil of California, has a West Coast base (San Francisco).

The picture is about the same in other businesses. New York shelters six of the top ten banking firms in the country. California has three, including San Francisco's BankAmerica, which is the biggest. But the combined assets in New York among the top ten are about double the combined assets in California.

All the top ten life insurance companies live outside the West Coast, and nine of them live on the East Coast between Boston, Newark, and New York. Five of the top ten diversified financial companies head-quarter along the rich toll roads between Connecticut and New York; only two of them sit near the freeways of the West Coast.

Only one of the top ten retailers is in California (Safeway Stores of Oakland). The East has four of the top ten and seven of the top twenty, compared to two of the top twenty in California. One of the top ten transportation firms is in California, and it isn't even an airline (Southern Pacific Railroad). Five of the top ten movers are from East Coast terminals, four of them in New York, and all four are airlines. Six of the top ten utilities live on the East Coast; the top three are in New York, led by American Telephone, which has more assets than the next seventeen utilities combined. One San Francisco utility and one Los Angeles utility make the top ten. The most populous state in the United States is still a puny power in relative terms of providing power.

More evidence comes from combining the *Fortune* survey with a Los Angeles *Times* survey of California companies done in the seventies.

Standard Oil of California, the only one among the national top twenty, is followed in the California lists by Lockheed of Burbank, a national member of the top thirty.

There are five oil companies in the California top ten, and three firms in the aerospace-systems business. Striking by its absence among the California top twenty is the entertainment industry, underlining once again the fact that amusement's power is more apparent than real.

Getty Oil is in the top ten California list, but only

in the top one hundred nationally. Carnation, the keepers of contented cows, make the California top twenty but do not qualify for *Fortune's* top one hundred. Del Monte, the giant food packer, is also in the California top twenty, but not even in the top one hundred fifty nationally.

The reality is that business is the East Coast's property, with only scattered power in the provinces. Government is unarguably an East Coast power source, with the federal policy makers and money changers at Washington, D.C. The media, while not the richest enterprises in America, are the businesses that most try to win friends and influence people. The media are also headquartered in the East.

All three national networks—NBC, CBS, and ABC—are at home in New York. Two of the top three publishers are in New York: Time, Inc. and McGraw-Hill; Times Mirror, publishers of the Los Angeles *Times,* is in California. The major book-publishing firms are in New York.

Spiro Agnew, a onetime student of American media, was not wrong when he accused the press of being in a mental bind bounded by New York and Washington. He wasn't wrong about their political bent being liberal, either—at least, liberal at the working level.

A later chapter will deal with how the media muck it up, in terms of East-West misunderstandings, but here I think it's important to locate power where it belongs.

When I first went to California as a correspondent for *Life* magazine, a friendly colleague said, "Don't worry, you'll be back." Assignment to a bureau outside

New York and west of Washington was assignment to Siberia or to show business, both considered remote hells beyond the mainstream of American news.

When I left Time, Inc., for Curtis Publishing because I didn't want to go back, because I wanted to stay in California, another colleague said, "Can you be happy out there? Writing about big boobs, land booms, and difficulties in breathing?"

Neither one of them was worried then about the impending deaths of *Life* and the *Saturday Evening Post*. And when I left the *Post* because the threat of moving east seemed imminent once more, Curtis Vice-President Clay Blair wanted to know whether thirty-two wasn't too early an age to put oneself to pasture. Blair had just carried the poor old *Post* from Philadelphia to New York, convinced that even Pennsylvania was a province and hence far removed from the center of the newsworthy universe.

This attitude of "show-biz Siberia in sunshine" seemed to dominate *The New York Times* when that dignified American messenger decided to begin a daily West Coast edition in the early sixties. The experts in production were enthused. The experts in advertising sales were excited; here was an opportunity to sell to the place where the people were moving to. But the editorial experts decided that a skeleton staff would be enough to cover whatever occurred on the West Coast.

The West Coast version of *The New York Times* appeared as a smaller version of the East Coast edition, with only a few splotches of local calamity and color. If an Atlantic City hurricane was the big story on the Eastern seaboard one day, it was also the major story for California. One wise reader likened the West Coast

NYT to the international edition of the *Herald Tribune*—a marvelous journal for New Yorkers who happened to be traveling and wanted news of home.

The paper failed for having Holland Tunnel vision, a sort of nearsightedness that considers everything west of the Hudson Tubes unimportant, to be underplayed.

Since the publishers and the networks operate out of New York, so do the writers and commentators. Tom Brokaw was an NBC anchorman in Los Angeles —intelligent, popular, serious. His masters invited him to become the network's White House correspondent. Brokaw had just bought a glassy new condominium on the beach at Venice, L.A. Meredith Brokaw was busy becoming her own California woman in education and environmental issues; she was happy and the Brokaw children were happy. The family agonized, but decided to leave California. A media man must be in Washington or New York, or nobody might ever hear from him again—much less notice him the next time a promotion came along.

The two types of novelists who've found appropriate homes in the West belong to the specialty schools of whodunit and whatisit: detective fiction and science fiction.

The East can accept such types because they support the fantasy notions about California. Never mind that Raymond Chandler accurately saw California after-hours undergrounds rarely exposed to the tiresome sunshine. Skip Ross Macdonald's private eye for sociology and a hero, Lew Archer, who really knows his overground. A detective is the logical descendant of the cowboy—Shane turned shamus who roams the remote range to conquer evil in his own simple way outside corporate law enforcement.

Ray Bradbury's vision of the future can also be forgiven, because it presents no immediate threat to Norman Mailer's cauliflower ear for dialogue, Philip Roth's view of contemporary masturbation, or Bernard Malamud's exquisite sense of urban alienation.

Joan Didion, too, can be accepted, with her extraordinary sensitivity to life along the Sacramento River or the Southern California freeway system. She's a woman, after all, and women are still about as far out on the periphery of publishing circles as crime writers and science-fictions writers.

Science fiction, above all other forms, is the expectable flower from the odd growth on California's unreal real estate. It is no accident, I think, that the world tolerates blobs that were born in the sprawl; the East takes California monsters for granted.

It is no accident, either, that three publications could become national weeklies with the similar names of *The New Yorker, New York,* and *New York Review of Books.* No journal out of Chicago, Los Angeles, or literarily pretentious San Francisco could ever hope to become an American institution by taking its title from its home town.

Such New York media, with advertisements for Bergdorf Goodman and Abercrombie & Fitch, also help maintain a commercial snobbism for the center of gravity. Some California people read *The New Yorker* for its ads more than its editorial quality, like peasants who pay court to the palace, obedient servants to the notion that what blows west from East must be the latest word in fashion style, acquisitive style—forget literary style.

I admit that we have a large percentage of people on the West Coast who wish they were on the opposite shore amidst all those French restaurants and Truman Capote cocktail parties. They believe only accidents of birth or corporate transfers dumped them so far from the font of the finer things in this world. If the United States ever works out a policy of people dispersion, such Californians would be the first to apply for passports to New York. But the worst cruelty they can imagine is to be sent, instead, to St. Louis, Cincinnati, or Forest Lawn's favorite butt, Detroit.

I admit that the East, along with money power and political power and a near media monopoly, has social status. The new condominiums at Fifth Avenue and Fifty-first Street have penthouse status at a mere $630,000 per unit. Nobody in California ever thought high-rise apartments would rise so high.

And I admit that all of that is all right with me. I like surviving in the least-liked city in America, by most media standards; there's a perverse pleasure in living in the number-one unloved one.

The East will continue to be the definitive seat of American substance so long as Americans continue to define importance in terms of money and power. So long as most Americans measure other Americans by how much they make or how much they influence, New York and Washington, D.C., will remain the capitals of the country. California will be for those people who couldn't care less—or certainly couldn't care as much—about being near the throne.

As would-be stars, Californians' hungers are more for fame than for power and money. As would-be stars, Californians resist the pull from the center of gravity. As would-be stars, they accept the idea of needing

83

outside producers or angels, and they would rather not compete with the money moguls.

But sometimes when they become stars, when their need to be unlisted shoves them further and further away from entertainment, because entertainment is their *business,* celebrity Californians begin to commute across the country. They are among the rich and powerful Americans who try to live two lives on two coasts, one foot in each of the best—or worst— possible worlds. Such cross-country commuters bring a new perspective to the polarity of this study. Their money allows them to pass above Chicago at forty thousand feet and come to earth only at the important ends of America: the eastern end, where the decisions are made that affect everyone, and the western end, where everyone wants to decide for self.

-VI-

Middle America Doesn't Matter

There are no Middle Americans, just mutations of East and West. Or, if there are Middle folk, they don't really matter. The life of these United States is pulled and shaped by what happens at both ends of the country.

Bostonians may have contempt for Californians, but they don't even bother looking down Back Bay noses at Terre Hauteans. Californians may be afraid of what New Yorkers can do to them, but they ignore Des Moines.

A small but extremely influential group of coastal Americans manages to keep one leg at either end of the country, a toe in each life style, stretched across three thousand miles by the pull of money.

Actors are among them. The Newmans, Joanne and Paul, keep house—or houses—at both extremes. They've lived in Connecticut, New York City, Beverly

Hills, and Malibu, at two or more of those addresses at the same time. Robert Mitchum has maintained a Maryland farm even while making films for a living. James Cagney lived on both shores before retiring to Massachusetts. Katherine Hepburn holds her lovely Main Line accent by never leaving the East completely.

Oddly, a British actor first made me aware of the way performers lead multiple lives. Rex Harrison came to Los Angeles in 1962 for the movie version of *My Fair Lady,* in which he recreated Professor Higgins for the last time. Harrison, then married to actress Rachel Roberts, rented a fairly fancy house in Hidden Valley, within twenty minutes' driving distance of the Warners Studios in Burbank. The street where he lived was secluded; the house was furnished in Overstuffed Opulence and came with a Romanesque swimming pool. But Harrison also liked the beach, which was too far from work for weekday commuting. So he rented a second house, in Malibu. The Harrisons lived in the Southern California hills from Monday through Friday, and moved to the Southern California beach from Saturday through Sunday.

The monthly payment for both homes was nearly two thousand dollars, and this was more than a decade ago. But the Harrisons also had a home in London. And another home in Italy, on the Mediterranean. Performers try to establish some stability in their nomadic lives by rooting in real estate. Shirley MacLaine, George Segal, and Jason Robards have held simultaneous mortgages at both sides of America.

Businessmen are also among them. George Scharffenberger, the president of City Investing Company, is probably prototypical. City Investing is a

two-billion-dollar conglomerate of insurance, development, motels, and manufacture, with headquarters in
New York. But President Scharffenberger is more at
home in California, on the Palos Verdes Peninsula,
where he owns twenty-one acres, a citrus grove, and a
stable of horses, and keeps bees.

Los Angeles writer Marshall Berges once asked the
tycoon how he happened to live so far from his work.
"When we were married," answered Scharffenberger
for *Home* magazine, "Marion and I agreed that we
should attempt to avoid, as far as possible, moves that
would be traumatic for a family, especially for the
children. Bear in mind that we had both worked for an
international company—ITT—that found it necessary
to move people around a great deal. Marion and I ob-
served the impact of all that moving on those families,
and we made up our minds to stay in one place. At one
point that meant I was able to fly home only on weekends, but as our company developed more and more
activities in the West, I've been able to spend a little
more time here."

Scharffenberger's commuting is heroic. He is in
the air ten to fifteen hours a week, logging more
monthly flight time than airline pilots do. He covers
some four hundred thousand miles a year, often in the
company-owned Jetstar. He wakes up at five-thirty or
six in the morning to begin his working day. He claims
that's not so terrible; he always was a poor sleeper.

The Scharffenbergers have been living this way
since 1959, when they pulled out of the East in order to
raise children and animals in the West.

I draw a line between the cross-country commuters of show business and business business. The

entertainers head west for work and east to soothe their sensibilities. The tycoons generally make their fortunes in the East and go west for warmer living conditions.

The beginnings of the movie business explain part of the actors' unease about life in California. They originally came to earn paychecks in film, while, as allowed earlier, their artistic pretensions stayed near the legitimate stage. Even the word "legitimate" has something to do with the taint of moving west to the movie business.

Writers who came to California later expanded the theme. Fitzgerald and Faulkner, each for his own reasons, found Southern California unfit for an artist. The movies were a fine place to make a killing, but Los Angeles was no place to live. The literary world that lives around the wings of the theater has traditionally damned California, Southern especially, for its lotus eaters and lack of hustle, for its sunglasses sham and its swimming sensuality. As if climates could corrupt art, and dry climates could leave art dessicated.

Newman or Robards or Segal, all with Broadway in their backgrounds, are not immune to such legends. Living in Los Angeles is a small sin against esthetics.

Businessmen don't have those hangups. The precedent for buying a West Coast home away from the cold was set decades ago. Easterners wealthy enough not to have to wait for retirement bought houses in San Francisco, Santa Barbara, and Pasadena. They commuted by train, seasonally, generally trying to spend the worst of the Eastern winter and the hottest portion of the Eastern summer in their second homes out West.

The jet made cross-continental commuting possible. A movie actor could move east every time he was between film engagements. And a businessman could come west for a rest whenever he had two consecutive days between appointments.

Another line can be drawn between the people who tend to tilt either way: Business commuters come to live in California after they have achieved big titles; stars tend to leave California after they have achieved big stardom. The rich can run away from the seat of their success.

The cross-country life is not easy for anyone. Even in the 747 era, a human body is in the air for five hours between New York and San Francisco, suffering the changes of three time zones, waiting at both ends with lines and luggage, enduring the inevitable unadvertised delays of magical sonic flightspeed.

They pay the full penalties of time and distance because they are afraid of leading half-lives by staying on one coast. Performers don't want to miss the new Broadway season or the pleasures of old-fashioned New England farm country. Executives don't want to skip the blooming western desert or the all-year tennis tournaments.

They can afford not to travel like mere tourists taking temporary joys in hotel rooms, but hotels are often used as houses by these two-sided citizens on either extreme.

The Beverly Hills Hotel, for instance, has cottages that can be rented on a permanent basis. It is a bulky but beautiful old hotel, sitting like a pink elephant in a rich residential neighborhood. At breakfast each morning in the Lanai Room, important people and posturing people do their eating and their business at the same time. There are telephones on long cords that can be brought to the tables. Breakfast in California is almost lunchtime in New York, so urgent deals must be made before the East Coast crowd has left the office for the regular two-hour, three-martini lunch. It's a unique balancing act: a forkful of Eggs Benedict in one hand and a telephone in the other. The Californian must time his activities, taking nourishment while the other coast is talking and swallowing just before it is his turn to speak.

The New York hotels facing Central Park offer comparable high-rising residential comforts for the West Coast celebrities who come to live rather than visit.

High passion surges through these people on both coasts. Most of them tend to view the original home as a place a person has to be and the other home as a place a person wants to be. One of the houses is kept out of a sense of necessity; the second house is held out of love. Rarely does a two-sided, twin-housed, double-bedded American admit to really liking both locations where he or she lives.

It is almost as if the more distance one can put between necessity and pleasure, the more one can appreciate the place of refuge. Whether desire lives in California or the East is unimportant; the price for such expensive multiple housekeeping is justified on emotional grounds: How difficult life would be if the alternative weren't always available on the opposite shore.

If the three ugly human drives are for power, fame, and money, the cross-country commuters are the people who have already achieved enough of all three to seek relief from their own ambition.

Hollywood stars tend to move east whenever they want to reestablish the legitimacy of their lives, as if they could deny their larger-than-life selves by changing locations.

The power brokers and money mongers of the East come to California whenever they need to reassure themselves that having a family or free time is important.

The American schizoids who live on both coasts help clarify the quintessential differences between East and West. The real accumulations of money and power are concentrated on the older shore. The illusions of fame, projected and magnified by the amusement business, reside in the West. I should call them "the real illusions of fame," because the celebrity of stars does exist. The boss of ITT may be much richer than Cary Grant and wield much more political influence than Jane Fonda, but how many people know his name or face or marital status?

If you want to make big money and big decisions, then you must join the Eastern team and learn all the plays. If you want to be a soloist—which is what stars are—and be recognized, then the West is where you may want to work. If you have the arrogance to be yourself, go west. If you have the optimism to sustain that arrogance, go west. If you make it at either end—the money coast or the amusement coast—then you'll be able to afford to do business at one end and seek refuge at the other.

Professional politicians (national stature) have to live Ping-Pong lives across the United States. The California variety has to work both coasts and, because of the distance involved, maintain dual residences.

91

One of them is Congressman Alphonzo Bell, Jr., a moderate Republican who represents a large stretch of the Southern California beaches as well as the rich residential community of Bel-Air. Bel-Air was named after Alphonzo Bell, Sr., who was a rancher, developer, and oilman.

Representative Bell has been living in Washington and California for the last four years—Monday through Thursday on Capitol Hill and Friday through Sunday at the family home in Hidden Valley—coincidentally, on the same street where Rex Harrison had his in-town house during *My Fair Lady*.

Bell's wife is actress Marian McCargo. Her film and television career is one reason why the Bells keep house on two coasts. The children—seven boys—are the other reason. When the Bells merged sons by previous marriages, it seemed important to give them a sense of continuity in California.

I happened to stop in at Bell's California office one Friday morning after he'd had a particularly complicated but not uncommon commute. His office was in the Federal Building at Westwood, a cold piece of bureaucratic architecture that suggests it was formed by a committee in Washington and then sent out here in pieces as a kit for reassembly. (Alas, that's not the case. Charles Luckman, once with Lever Brothers in New York and now with his own design firm in Los Angeles, was the creator. The Federal Building is one of Luckman's least-distinguished projects, as if he had unhappy memories of the way government works in the East.) Bell was saying "you can never depend on the House and Senate" because there's no way to predict adjournment among so many members who want oral gratification from each debate.

Bell's regular routine is to leave Dulles International on American Airlines' 5:55 flight Thursday evening. That means quitting the Capitol at about 4:30. He doesn't keep a car in Washington any more, not since he rented an apartment within one walking block from the office. Usually he bums a ride to Dulles with another California congressman who's going west for the weekend, often Democrat Ed Roybal or Democrat Gus Hawkins.

But on this particular Thursday the House was arguing a military authorization bill that would have increased aid to South Vietnam. Bell was opposed, and it seemed important to vote. He heard the debate drag on beyond 4:30, and he asked an aide to cancel the 5:55 reservation; could he have space on the 7:15 flight?

He could. But the debate continued. A page came up to his seat on the floor with a message from the aide: Should they cancel the 7:15? They had to. The aide searched around airlines schedules and found something that left Washington National Airport at 8:55. It stopped in Chicago. It stopped again in Kansas City. It did not get in to California until 1:40 A.M. on Friday.

It would have to do. "There were no meals on the plane," said Bell. "Anyone leaving at eight fifty-five was assumed to have had dinner." Worse, when the plane landed in Chicago Bell discovered he was unable to walk to the snack bar, order, and be back within thirty minutes. Distances are too great at O'Hare Field. The congressman finally had a midnight snack in

93

Kansas City, having missed lunch because of an education bill and dinner and two airplanes because of a military bill. Bell had to hit Middle America. It fed him. He was home by 2:30 A.M., which was 5:30 A.M. on a watch still timed to Washington.

Coming west is easier than going east, when a cross-country resident has to set his or her clocks—internal and external—ahead. Alphonzo Bell's preferred flight eastward leaves at 3:45 P.M. That at least allows him most of the day in California and almost a whole night's sleep in Washington before rising at 7:30 the next morning. The morning flights from California kill a whole day. The night flights steal sleeping time.

If the Bells have something important to do in Los Angeles on a Sunday evening, then Alphonzo catches the famous "red eye," the jet that leaves California at 10:35 P.M. and arrives in Washington at dawn, Eastern time. The congressman can cab directly from Dulles to the office and start his working day.

Some veterans of the dual-residence experience have developed the ability to sleep in planes, limousines, taxicabs, and terminals. Bell's talents are only mediocre. "If it's a crowded plane, I can't. Even if I were to travel first class, I couldn't pull out the middle armrest and stretch out. I've learned a little bit about sleeping sitting down, though. Sometimes Marian will ask me what I'm doing at the table and discover that I've been asleep."

Outdoorsman Bell looks like a congressman sent to the Capitol by central casting: white hair over wide smile over pinstripe tailoring over calf-high boots. "Staying out here in California," he said, "suits our picture better; it certainly suits my political picture better. When I lived in Washington, it was almost like being a Washington congressman; I didn't know the issues well in California, I wasn't really with it."

He talked about leading two different lives on the two coasts: "Back here I'm trying to satisfy my constituents; back there I'm concentrating on legislation. Out here I have a tendency to socialize with people, to accept speaking dates or put out a little charm—whatever's left of it. In Washington, people say, 'We're having a convention of bankers at the Hilton—why don't you come by,' and I say, 'No, I'll see you in my office.' "

He usually flies coach between homes, which means about $1,500 a month in jet fares alone. The government allows congressmen thirty-three trips per two-year term. The government also pays for Bell's cross-country habit when he has to attend committee hearings in California. And because Bell still has an interest in the family oil company, most of the rest of his flying can be charged to business.

I asked whether Washington denigrates its congressmen from California. On the contrary, he said. "California, being the biggest delegation, is a threat. If the Californians get together on an issue, then there's a real danger of passage. If New York and California manage to get together, then you've got a pretty sure thing."

Bell had just been involved with a school-aid bill that helped the rest of the country at New York's expense; because New York spends so much more per pupil than any other state in the union, it did not benefit from the federal funding. California, by contrast, is close to the national average in education expenditure. So California profited by the measure.

Bell admits that such results are not exactly fair or fitting. California, the most populous state, the richest agricultural state, should be spending almost what New York—the center of gravity—spends per pupil in public schools. While the cost of living may be slightly higher in wetter, more wintry New York, the expense for learning should be about equal.

But California does not always do well by its young people. It may worship their youth. It may be jealous of their beauty. But the least-content Californians turn out to be those people who grew up there, as we shall soon see.

-VII-

Aging Your Act

The age of discontent in California starts at about junior high, and the quality of misery grows right along with the bearer through high school and into college.

One of the ironies of contemporary America is that Californians worship youth but youth tends to detest California. The young people who grow up on the West Coast have everything in the eyes of their parents: beauty, truth, opportunity, and easy access to the beaches. In their own eyes and in their own words, young people see California as fucked over—fucked over by over-development, fucked over and paved over in asphalt and plastic, fucked over from materialism.

California is where the student revolution started in the mid-sixties, born in Berkeley by the Free Speech Movement, which made it possible for publishers to print such terms as "fucked over" in polite pages.

97

California is where a massive rock concert ended in death, at Altamont, where flower children were beaten by goons wielding billiard cues.

California is where dropping out and heavy doping moved from poverty areas into the nicest neighborhoods because upper-middle young people didn't know what to do with themselves under the sun amidst so much affluence.

I think it's safe to say that children who grow up in California have a keen sense of utopia. They quickly learn to despise or demean their current conditions because they don't know any worse. "Spoiled" is a fair word. But so is "disillusioned." California is a whole state of illusion, because even a promised land cannot live up to the promises of American refugees who came to raise families out of the cold.

Teen-agers sit around the San Fernando Valley complaining about the boredom of life in a bedroom community. They hate the new high-rises. They have contempt for the new density. They abhor the omnipresent automobile, often ignoring the hypocrisy in having one. They dream of moving north, to the Bay Area, where urbanity and sophistication are supposed to prevail.

College-age young people sit around San Francisco complaining about the pressures of life under a peninsular mentality. They hate high-rises, density, and automobiles. They dream of moving north, to Oregon or British Columbia, where rural communities and root values are supposed to prevail.

If the people who came to California were indeed refugees from the East, their children are the next generation of refugees—ready to claim that surfing and sexual freedom and quadraphonic speaker systems are not enough. These malcontents have rarely seen the real high-rise as it closes off the sky on Wall Street, real density as it slams shut life in the subways, or real traffic jams as they turn the Jersey shore into one steel wall.

Their self-loathing is sometimes funny. A few academic quarters ago, a humor magazine at the University of California, Berkeley, ran a cartoon strip about two young lovers who met on campus, shared aspirations and pillows, decided their passion was so strong that even marriage—the most radical new relationship of all—was appropriate. The night before the wedding the young man said he had a terrible secret he had to tell his love: He was from Southern California, specifically from Los Angeles. She confessed to having exactly the same sin in her past. They cried, parted, and never saw each other again.

The moves, from Southern to Northern California, from Northern California to out of state, are natural enough in the context of young people having to renounce their parents and leave home. In the East, it may be sufficiently symbolic to take an apartment three subway stops away from the family residence and proclaim independence. In the state of illusion and vast distances, establishing individuality may require leaving California.

The young people of the East, rich and poor, are disciplined by the urban system in which they live. Trains have schedules. Buses stop at marked corners. Restaurants fill up at certain hours. Shops are open certain days, normally not on Sundays.

California isn't like that. The young people of the

West can almost shape their lives to suit, especially if they own a vehicle that can carry them anywhere at whim. California is home of the all-night market, Sunday shopping, and twenty-four-hour breakfasts in coffee shops. California is easy to rebel against because everything, including disaffection, is convenient. New York is not so easy.

Youth's alternative to fucked over is usually funk, probably best described as frays and fringes, anything old—or anything that looks old—in furniture, clothing, human hair, or artwork. The Now Generation has deliberately become the Then Generation in California. Newness is bad karma, usually made of plastic. Thenness is luxurious, manufactured out of the fabric of nostalgia. Funk is so commercially successful that, in the spring of 1974, California shoe shops were showing brand-new denim sandals, with frays right out of the factory, and clothing stores were featuring jeans with fade marks made on the assembly line.

Such immediate economic integration of youth's individuality infuriates the more anguished young adults. What could be worse than to see the materialists take the protests of the anti-materialists and manufacture them into material success? It's as if the parents, instead of ordering haircuts, let their own hair out and down to ape their children.

Of course, that's exactly what happens in California. Elders consistently take their cues from youngers, especially in matters of superficial fashion and skin decoration. When young boys went back to jeans, so did their fathers. When girls stopped wearing lipstick, so did their mothers. If California's young people have to

100

make big moves to declare their maturity, part of the reason is that California's old people are constantly embracing the little rebellions and turning them into middle-class style.

There is a California middle age of discontent that raises vanity to its highest power in the United States. The movies have been blamed for making Americans, especially Southern California Americans, obsessed with trying to look young, to wear perpetual suntans, to sport eternally unsagging chests, to have forever flat bellies, and to walk aroung in ever-unwrinkled skin.

Any East-West observer will grant apparent differences between contemporaries on each coast. The California women look taller, tanner, and trimmer than their Eastern relatives. California men enjoy a similar advantage.

But more than movies are involved. The sunshine seems to demand such vanity, as if the pursuit of pleasure in the outdoors requires an athletic shape.

Eastern winters demand the opposite: bulk. Body bulk helps against the wet and cold, just as a big coat does. The big coat conceals a fair amount of fat, anyway; a Bostonian swathed in wool cap and camel's hair doesn't have to be self-conscious about his or her body on the streets. A Washingtonian who can't swim in the wintertime has little reason for concern about his or her appearance in bathing attire from October to June.

Californians are used to exposure—decent and indecent—on a year-round basis. They can dress for swimming, tennis, or golf any day of the year. They can dress for those activities even if they don't perform them. A woman in a bikini squeezing grapefruit at the supermarket is no surprise. A man in track shorts without a top will raise no eyebrows in downtown Beverly Hills.

Weather shapes Southern Californians. So does their sense of removal. The psychology that shoved these people away from the East included a need not to be like, look like, or age like their parents. They came to California as young spirits, and they refuse to recognize themselves as anything older. If parents were wrong, then nobody wants to be a parent. Movie directors wear short pants because short pants confirm their senses of childhood.

Adult Californians jog, play tennis, do calisthenics. We use bodies by Fisher for errands and business. our own bodies with fear and love.

The line between nutty and narcissism and superb self-care is fuzzy, but there are whole industries in California catering to either drive.

We have the health-food industry, which has organic compounds for every occasion and food supplements which guard against all strains of hypochondria. Fruits and vegetables in health-food stores cost about 33 percent more than similar stuff in regular stores, partly because of the manure in which they presumably grow better.

We have the beauty-salon industry, which offers head-to-toe styling for men and women, with haircuts that brush up to fifty dollars apiece and foot massages that begin at about five dollars. An afternoon in a salon like Aida Grey's in Beverly Hills is an easy eighty dollars for hairwork, facial, massage, and dyeing of eyelashes. Men and women dye their eyelashes dark in

California, because the sun bleaches them during all that tennis and bicycling.

We have the spa industry, which operates on a day basis in the downtowns and weekly basis in such opulent hideaways as the Golden Door near Escondido. A week at the Door, room and board and calisthenics included, costs more than nine hundred dollars. Reservations must be made months in advance, because the hunger for dieting is constant. A few years ago, on assignment rather than obsession, I attended a men's week at the Golden Door. The clients included a movie producer, an oil tycoon, a San Francisco publisher, a professional football coach, and two financial consultants from the East. The astonishing fact about my fellow classmates was that almost none of them was fat—flabby, perhaps, but in better shape than the average man in the street of between thirty-five and seventy years. The term "fat farm" is used in New York for places where gross people take off gross amounts of weight. The California spa, in contrast, is a place where well-proportioned people improve their proportions. Incidentally, none of the California men was embarrassed by a daily massage, an herbal wrap, or a pedicure. The San Franciscan even had his toenails painted.

We have the plastic-surgery industry, which operates expensive parts shops to perfect faces, breasts, eyes, chins, stomachs, rumps, and even ears. Eyes are big these days; women have decided not to allow themselves the weathering of crows'-feet, smile lines, or wrinkled lids.

We have the diet industry under doctors' care,

with a wide variety of prescribed cures for fatness that can involve daily visitations to the doctor's office for an injection in the rear or a pill in the mouth.

Easterners tend not to talk about physical func- or personal artifices. Californians dote on such discussions. Women will tell you about the silicone they carry within their chests. Men will admit to dyeing their hair or having hair transplants. The sin in California is not the lengths to which one will go in order to be beautiful; the sin is in allowing oneself to be not-beautiful, in permitting natural aging, in being indifferent to surface appearance.

I said the distinction between good health and narcissism was fuzzy; I confess that my neighbor Californians err on the side of pampering the outer person. Mirror images mean too much to them.

Being old, honestly old, is more difficult on the West Coast for such reasons. There are working prejudices against the elderly in California, a form of bigotry we are beginning to call "ageism." Middle-aged adults turn away from their elders, to copy adolescents or to study themselves. Having a septuagenarian parent around the house is an embarrassment for some, an agonizing embodiment of the future for others.

Retirement homes and senior-citizen communities are all over the West. Again, weather is only the easy excuse. Keeping the elders out of sight is also part of the story. A culture that worships youth can treat age as a dread disease, something that can be caught, something that suggests the aged have committed an immoral act merely by being.

Old people live in New York, Washington, and Boston as visible figures in the urban landscape. In Los

Angeles and San Francisco, only the old poor seem to appear. The old people who can afford decent housing tend to be in the pasture communities, possibly content with one another, but once-removed from the everyday life of the downtowns.

The old have other problems in the West. A lack of mass transportation in Southern California may mean an aged person has no mobility. In the culture spawned by the mating of car and driver on endless roadbed, the grandparent who can no longer perform the automotive act is a kind of cripple. A shortage of neighborhood parks compounds the cruelty. California was so busy speculating, sprawling, and booming that little land was preserved as open green space, especially down south. Los Angeles may have the most moderate weather of any big city in the country, but it has the least amount of public sitting room for basking in that weather. And the California habit of resisting community, resenting organization, works more hardship on the elderly. Senion-citizen centers are established almost grudgingly, as if the cities wished the churches would provide all the social life, the intellectual stimulation, and the human concern that old people need.

I keep meeting elderly people who say they came to Los Angeles for their health but not their happiness. The same respect for individual privacy that protects young people in California is an obstacle for old people, who need propinquity and company. Californians are friendly in the same way they are attractive: on the surface.

The newest age bloc in the West runs from late teens to middle age and is most easily marked by its characteristic singleness. The unmarrieds have made separate and segregated lives for themselves in apartment complexes, in bars, in vacation clubs.

Single swingers can live and play and eat without ever seeing an old person, a child, or even a married contemporary. They are a species apart, as if they suddenly popped into California from another planet, without fathers or mothers or kid sisters. Their mores don't always resemble those of the rest of the population.

Confirmed singles have made casualness a strict code, carrying surface friendliness to surface relationships. Meeting someone in a piano bar is good. Sleeping with someone without admitting emotional involvement is also good. Having expectations of someone is bad. Such refusals to form profound or prolonged relationships exist all over the world, but they achieve ritualistic performance in California because the singles stay so singularly apart from the larger community.

They seem to enjoy their part of the provinces. So do the majority of marrieds in the traditional bedroom communities of San Mateo, Santa Monica, and La Jolla. The adults who don't worship California are the youngest adults and oldest adults. I think that has something to do with lack of experience among the young and too much experience in other places among the old.

-VIII-

Before the Sex, Drive

The three couples decided to eat at Yamato's, an excellent Japanese restaurant in Century City, a heap of high-rises just beyond the border of Beverly Hills.

Alan Atkins would have to come from his office, downtown. He would drive some fifteen miles and meet the others at the restaurant. Alicia Atkins would proceed from the family home, in Pacific Palisades —another fifteen miles in the opposite direction.

Bill Bjork had a sales meeting in San Francisco that afternoon; his car was at the airport. He'd fly down in time to pick up his automobile and drive directly to the restaurant—about twelve miles. Betty Bjork would take her car down Beverly Glen to Yamato's. Century City is only six miles from home, but there's no public transportation from the Bjorks' to the city in the suburbs.

Calvin Carp was finishing his film at the Burbank Studios; if he went a few miles out of his way on the Ventura Freeway, he could go home, shower, and pick up Carly Carp. They could arrive in one car.

The Atkinses, the Bjorks, and the Carps came to dinner in five cars, for a total round-trip distance of more than one hundred miles. Each driver also had to pay the parking attendant one dollar for the privilege of storing all these automobiles during the meal. When dinner was done, the same five automobiles with the same five drivers carried the married people home again—almost as if each person were single. Calvin Carp had had a little too much sake with his dinner, and Carly Carp tried to talk him into letting her do the driving. He refused. They argued all the way back to Encino. The only couple that traveled together argued.

That is a typical California social evening, involving nearly as many automobiles as human beings.

Alan Atkins's business life is almost as bizarre in the asocial terms of the automobile. There are days when he sees no one, or almost no one, from the time he rises until he goes to bed.

The radio alarm clock goes off at 6:30 A.M. in the Atkins home atop Marquez Knolls. Not even Lohman and Barkley, radio's dawn Theater of the Absurd, disturb Alicia's sleep. The Atkins children, Ayn and Abel, do not have to get up for school until 7:30. A bus picks them up. There's no such bus for Alan. He tried car pooling for a month during the Arab embargo, but the men who live near his house don't work anywhere near his office, and the other people in the office don't live within ten miles of the Atkins home.

So Alan is alone, listening to Lohman and Barkley for company as the sun rises to stripe the sky over the Santa Monica Mountains. He toasts an Orrowheat sourdough English muffin, pours a glass of Minute Maid frozen orange juice, and boils water for a cup of freeze-dried Maxim coffee. Over breakfast, he reads Jim Murray's sports column. There never seems to be time for more than sports and the stock reports. He'll try to finish the paper down at the office, but the telephone usually won't let him. He'll catch the evening news on television, and that will be enough notice of the world's catastrophes for another day. Alicia always has time to read in the mornings. She's less driven, but better informed; maybe that's why housewives in the Movement think they're so damn smart.

Alan stacks his dish, glass, and cup in the sink, grabs his pale blue polyester doubleknit jacket, and pulls the damn Toronado out of the garage—damn Toronado because he bought it just before the energy crisis, and the car uses a gallon of gasoline every nine miles, every ten miles if he's on the freeways cruising. A few more bucks and he could have bought a Mercedes, but who knew? Alicia's Mazda is supposed to be an economy car, but it uses a gallon every sixteen miles. Air conditioning and automatic transmission are the trouble.

Alan drives down to Sunset Boulevard, across to the San Diego Freeway, down the San Diego to the Santa Monica Freeway, across the Santa Monica to the Harbor freeway, up the Harbor to the Sixth Street exit, and over to his office in the United California Bank tower. On an easy morning, the drive takes less than an hour. On this morning, with jam-ups all along the

Santa Monica and a crash on the Harbor, he is at the wheel for seventy-four minutes. He sees no one during that time.

He approaches the tower through the basement garage, leaves his Toronado, and enters the elevator. Sometimes there are other office workers in the elevator. Today, there are none.

Atkins is aware of, but does not see, the receptionist on his floor. His secretary is not at her desk. Coffee break, probably, because there are some messages already stabbed through the spindle next to his telephone. He spends the morning returning calls, reading the report from the field representative, and getting ready to write his own proposal for the possible HUD grant. He buzzes his secretary and asks her to have an avocado-and-alfalfa sandwich, on wheat, sent up to his desk; he won't have time to go out today.

He works until 6, sweeps the proposal into his attaché case, knowing he won't read it at home but thinking he ought to, and elevators down to his car again. The drive home is the same as the drive in that morning. The sun is in his eyes again, because the sun is always in the direction he's heading. The car radio is off halfway home; he's already heard the cycle of news on KFWB. He's read communications from a couple of bumper strips along the way, for and against impeachment. He's noted a few personalized license plates, including I WUV IT on a new Mercedes. And he's amused to realize that the Santa Monica Freeway warning signs are no longer operating; they used to carry such inane electronic messages as NORMAL SLOWING. If slowing were normal, there'd be no need to warn people about it in advance.

Atkins pulls into the garage at 7:03, opens the front door, and greets Abel, who only nods in passing. Ayn is in the family room watching *I Love Lucy* on Channel 11. Alicia is in the kitchen, feeding Axel his daily ration of Alpo. Axel jumps on him—the heartiest encounter he's had in thirteen hours.

Contrast Atkins's commute with that of one of his cousins on the East Coast, who rides in from Scarsdale every day. The Scarsdale man is driven to the train station by his wife—only one car in the family. The Scarsdale man stands on the platform with a bunch of his buttoned-down neighbors, each carrying a folded copy of *The New York Times*—which will be read on the thirty-five-minute ride to New York City.

If the Scarsdale cousin doesn't talk to his fellow travelers, he is aware of their existence. He is also aware of Westchester, the Bronx, and Harlem as the train proceeds. Harlem is particularly apparent, because the tracks are elevated at One hundred twenty-fifth Street, the train stops there to let passengers off, and the tenements are at eye level with the commuters. A person can see slum life simply by looking through the windows on a summer day.

The Scarsdale man switches from train to subway at Grand Central Station. It is impossible to ignore people on the subway, to sit across from their faces and not see pain or joy or fatigue. Bodies bump, bodies shove, bodies smell. The subway is a bruising experience, but it is also a place where people gather, by necessity, and absorb the thumps of urban life. Well-to-do people, ne'er-do-well people, and poor people share the same space.

The New York sidewalks are also shared transportation areas. The Scarsdale man climbs up out of the subway station and walks four blocks to his office, on Lexington Avenue. He must, for his own safety if not his own comfort, be alert to other pedestrians and their elbows. He enters the building at ground level, with other walking people. The elevator is always crowded. More bodies bump, make concessions to one another.

Alan Atkins has no such intimacy. Safety on the freeways means looking straight ahead. Turning to see scenery or drivers in adjacent lanes is a perilous mistake. Many of the freeway routes are cut below human life or raised above residential life anyway. Californians realized they never had seen Watts before Watts burned; it was right off the Harbor Freeway, but nobody was looking; nobody really could look unless a driver specifically decided to leave the mainstream of traffic and visit Watts. Atkins sees no people, just bumpers and belching exhausts, the gaseous wastes of other automobiles.

The commuters of Philadelphia, Baltimore, and New Haven may not want to be amidst people, but they have little choice. Daily familiarity may breed contempt; it also forces understanding and some degree of sensitivity to the way other people live.

The East, I confess, trains a certain appreciation for the human condition between Scarsdale and Forty-second Street.

The West insulates citizens against such appreciation, by surrounding the affluent with eight-cylinder, four-barrel steel machines. Almost every man is an island in California, if he can afford it.

Almost every woman does her errands in automotive armor.

When the gasoline crunch became a test of human patience in the winter of '74, New Yorkers seemed to cope better than Californians. They were used to crowds in New York. They had already survived subway strikes, garbage strikes, school strikes, and a memorable power blackout. Californians, meanwhile, were unprepared for scheduling themselves to urban systems, adjusting themselves to urban breakdowns. Californians pulled monkey wrenches, crowbars, and guns at gas stations when they couldn't fill up and flee in the style to which they had been accustomed.

There is another way to view the Atkins experience, however: California sprawl permits unworry as well as insularity. Fear is not something Atkins takes to and from the office every day. California apartment houses do not have nearly as many armed guards as New York buildings do. California taxicabs do not have bullet-proof shields between driver and passenger. California homeowners do not live behind a fortress of bolted doors, barred windows, and burglar alarms. Some Californians, more wary than most, do keep guns in their nighttables. They do not carry them, however.

The car has been both the chicken and the egg for life in Los Angeles. It caused the freeways that created the routes that allowed the distances that spilled the sprawl that subdivided the land that became the house that Atkins built. And once the car had hatched such possibilities—the single driver from the single-family residence rolling by his own time clock—a whole culture and an entire economy were enslaved to make more eggs. Freeways were free, to encourage driving at state roadbuilding expense. Gasoline used to be cheap and plentiful. Parking was more than ample; in the sixties more than two thirds of downtown Los Angeles was paved in the herringbone patterns of car lots. California was the best customer in the country for Detroit and for the petroleum industry. And the eggs are still among us: Of the 124 million vehicles registered in the United States in 1973, 13.5 million were in California. California has about 10 percent of the people in America; it owns about 11 percent of the cars. If that isn't boggling enough, there is more than one vehicle in California for every two people; no wonder we rarely see more than one person in an automobile on the freeway system.

Insanity, of course. A longtime enemy of the automobile, architectural critic Lewis Mumford, told a 1974 audience that America was already in a dark age and that Los Angeles had destroyed its urban spaces with cars. But he missed one point. Los Angeles, the Rorschach sprawl, is a multi-celled urban animal. Those old bedroom communities—Van Nuys, Westwood, San Pedro—have grown up to become small cities in their own right, offering commerce, government offices, health care, and other urban services. Now, if there's a blackout in downtown Los Angeles, life will continue almost as usual for the population. If there's a failure in downtown Philadelphia, Boston, or New York, the population is almost paralyzed. The sprawl could be salvation for California, even if California must find a new vehicle for getting around in it—one that doesn't produce smog or depend on Arabs.

114

A car is expensive, inefficient for the movement of masses, and an extraordinarily wasteful user of space when it's sitting unused in a garage or lot. But the roadbeds born of the unholy marriage between commuter and internal-combustion machine are not necessarily a mistake. They are the connectors and dispersers that could carry better devices for carrying Californians long distances in short times. California turns out to be lucky, because not every working man must be on Manhattan Island.

Sprawl prevented density, a fate portending urban death. The entire argument here is about preserving the West from the frustrating density of the East.

The Californian as refugee has already built peculiar provisions for privacy as a hedge against density. There are more walls and fences around California homes than weather would seem to call for. Some residents suggest that the walls are merely ornamental homage to California's Spanish heritage. Bosh. California has every architectural style ever built anywhere on 'earth, and none triumphs. Some other residents say that the fences are to screen skinnydippers in private pools. Bosh some more. Californians, suited or not, rarely use their pools. The grape-stake fence has become a symbol of the unlisted man in the single-family residence, behind which all residents want to enclose their personal lives from the community. Remember, people came to California to escape relatives, towns, traditions, and neighborhood involvements. They wanted to uncommit, and a wall is a visible way to avoid becoming too close to the other families in the cul-de-sac.

They have been extremely successful at staying

115

behind their own fences. California has one of the poorest records in the country for per-capita charity giving. In Los Angeles, big tycoons have to be bullied into assuming chairmanship of the annual United Way drive. An attempt in the sixties to induce participation from Southern Californians in the development of a plan for planless Los Angeles was a mammoth failure.

The Bay Area is better than Southern California in terms of community commitment. Citizens' organizations and regional government, particularly as applied to environmental causes, have been powerful in the San Francisco surround. But organizing around a political party is rare in any part of the state. Mobilizing people to support a popular cause often achieves more resentment than results.

The grape-stake-fence mentality of Southern California has been a major reason for failures of master planning, for the lack of mass transit, for the establishment of nearly eighty separate cities within the confines of the Los Angeles County. Everybody wants to be left alone. Only when an immediate neighborhood is threatened do the citizen troops muster—to try to prevent a new freeway from crossing back yards in La Canada; to try to prevent Occidental Oil from hoisting a drill rig in Pacific Palasades; to try to prevent a new tract development in Benedict Canyon. Southern Californians rouse themselves when something is about to happen close to home, usually in an anti organization.

But there's another way to look at non-involvement, too. I remember the pressures put upon neighbors in New York: to join a house of worship; to enroll

116

the children in a Sunday school or a Cub Scout troop or a Bluebird nest; to be active in the PTA; to do a dozen other things that all meant you must belong.

Belonging may mean community—coerced conformity.

Students of contemporary American life love to write about community being lost as the nuclear family, the neighborhood church, and the nearby general store disappear or disintegrate. California is usually cited as the state where disintegration has reached its highest power. The car takes the blame again.

And there is some truth to that complaint. The family that has almost one automobile for every member of driving age is a family of radial spokes in which almost everyone goes his or her own way. But I was relieved to reach California and feel free not to belong. I was delighted that my children weren't taunted for not going to Sunday school. I was elated to contribute money to the PTA without having to give time.

We could form communities of interest instead, using the automobile. A community of interest, in the California sense, is literally an association based on mutual enthusiasms rather than propinquity or geography. When a crowd of well-to-do and do-good women from the enclave of Beverly Hills decided they wanted to help provide day-care services for the ghetto, Neighbors of Watts was formed, and a community of interest was successfully established. The women gave time and money and commitment. When a horde of UCLA alums meet for weekly picnics at Exposition Park before every home football game, each coming by separate car, that's another kind of community of interest. Such people see each other as often as immediate neighbors do, but the bond is shared pleasure, not nearness.

Communities of interest have a kind of flexibility that geographic communities don't. They come and go based on the desires of the members. Neighbors of Watts, for instance, lost some neighbors once the day-care center had been established and the day-to-day operations were in capable black hands. The women who dropped out went on to new enthusiasms, joining new do-good efforts in other fields. There's usually no stigma when someone in a California community of interest moves on to another interest. But when someone drops out of a neighborhood organization in the East, the pressures are often reapplied.

A few years after coming to Southern California and moving into a middle-class home in the middle-level hills of middle-income Sherman Oaks, I discovered that we had a whorehouse among us.

"Discovered" is, in truth, too active a verb. The revelation was thrust upon me at three A.M. one morning when our doorbell was rung. I stumbled to the front of the house and saw a man's shadow through the translucent glass next to the front door. "Whaddya want," I shouted, unwilling to meet him face-to-face at that hour. "I have an appointment with Miss Brown," he said. Miss Brown, I said, doesn't live here. Oh, he said, and then apologized, explaining that he must want another house.

For the next several weeks I paid more than usual attention to that stucco house. Automobiles came and went at all hours on all evenings. Always men emerged from the cars. Usually they drove off within an hour or two.

I knew that there were three women living in that house, but I never saw any of them—although I tried peeking over the grape-stake fence into their back yard, I walked the dog up to the cul-de-sac more often than the dog needed walking, and I worked at home and was as available for lending a cup of flour as any housewife.

The whorehouse, meanwhile, continued to run efficiently. Aside from that one mistake, I was never disturbed by it. Our children were unaware of anything unusual. And we couldn't have asked for quieter neighbors. The live-and-let-live spirit of California captivated me; how romantic to have three prostitutes in the midst of two-car garages and tricycles.

The neighborhood probably would have lived happily ever after had not one of the other neighbors up the street become roaring drunk one night and, in a frenzy of lower-class lust, banged on the whores' door. They refused to admit him. Possibly because he had no previous appointment. Possibly because he was so obviously inebriated.

The drunk was furious. He went home and had another couple of drinks. Then he returned to the cathouse and pulled the rural mailbox out of the front yard. He rang the bell again. When one of the women opened the door, he hurled the mailbox at her. The woman promptly called the police, risking her illegitimate career out of legitimate fear for her own safety. The police arrested the man, apparently without questioning the women about any business on the premises.

When the unrequited patron came home on bail, he tried to enlist all us neighbors in a counterattack against the cathouse. He went door-to-door talking

119

about the evils of having whores on the block, about the terrible influences prostitutes can be on children, about how our property values were being ruined by allowing a madam in our midst. Some of the neighbors had known about the house but hadn't been bothered by it. Some had an idea about how the house slept odd-hour visitors but never pursued their suspicions. A few were shocked to hear what had been happening; they'd never noticed anything unusual. Hardly any of them wanted to join the middle-class man in his attempt to have the women evicted, especially after the middle-class man talked about owning a gun and how he would personally order the women out of the neighborhood if the police didn't do it first.

The irony was that, by trying to rouse the cul-de-sac and by his own disorderly behavior, he became our neighborhood disturbance. A madman was more dangerous than a madam. We were all content when we were uninvolved. He created trouble. We refused to become a community of interest. He soon moved away. The whores lasted longer. I don't know what eventually happened to any of the principals.

I eventually moved away myself, to a street where there were fewer houses and less opportunities for relationships with neighbors or their patrons. Interesting, the way we talk of places to live as "streets" in our culture; we identify home by how you get there.

And for adventurous Californians the street, or freeway, has suddenly become a place to react against the insularity, the unsociability, and the invisibility of community. These adventurers are using the vehicle of California privacy, the private car, to risk relationships against all odds of safety and sanity. Within one

120

week during the summer of '74, three writers were describing the phenomenon, each in his or her own terms.

Columnist Jack Smith dealt with the dangers of husband and wife both being on the road at the same time. An insurance agent identified as Charley said there were frequent claims made by married man and married woman who had collided with each other. Smith's account of Charley's horror stories included the case of the double-dented husband:

A man came home early from work one evening and pulled into his driveway. Even as he was arriving, his wife was racing from the house to the garage by a connecting passage, unaware that her mate had just stopped in front of the garage. "Before the husband knew what was happening," wrote Smith, "his wife was into reverse and backing up with a roar. There was a crash." Charley was the insurance agent who arranged for the repairs of both cars, and his story picked up again when the couple went to the shop and reclaimed their automobiles. He started home in his car. She started home in hers. On Vine Street she made a sudden stop for a traffic light. He was right behind her, but he was ogling a passer-by and didn't see the sudden stop quickly enough. There was a crash. They went back to the body shop.

Freelance writer Ann Lapides told the story of her innocent pickup by a pickup truck: "I'm not sure when the new green pickup tucked in behind me in the fast lane on the Hollywood Freeway. Somewhere around Vermont Avenue I realized that he had been there for a while, and that I felt comfortable about it."

He was still there after she had moved from the

121

Hollywood to the Ventura Freeway, and he was still there "as we negotiated the crisscrossing chaos west of the San Diego interchange." Lapides decided that the pickup driver was an excellent driver, because his patterns were so like hers. "I'd been thinking of him all along as a 'he' because trucks, to me, seem masculine per se. Now I could glimpse just enough of the driver to see that he was, indeed, a 'he.' "

A New York woman would have been terrified by then. Not a California Lapides. The two vehicles remained close for more than thirty miles, until she pulled off the freeway at the western end of the San Fernando Valley. The man in the green pickup waved good-bye. They have not met since.

"If I tried to tell people I'd had a meaningful experience on the freeway," continued Lapides, "they'd think I was out of my gourd. Yet the warm feeling persisted. Maybe establishing a meaningful—if transitory—relationship with a pickup truck was not so remarkable. Maybe it happens all the time, and people are just too embarrassed to report it. Perhaps any given freeway, at any given moment, is fairly teeming with Datsuns relating to Oldsmobiles, Mustangs getting it on with Volvos, Mercedes-Benzes cozying up to Chrysler Imperials. Consider the possibilities."

I did. And I was about to believe my respected writer friend Ann Lapides was as out of her gourd as only a car-driven Californian can be. But then came William Wilson's story, a few days later.

Art critic Bill Wilson has always had a soft spot, in his head and in his heart, for the automobile. He's always understood my New York friend who insists that California is the only place where the automobile is an important, beloved member of the family. Now Wilson insists he's been in the midst of auto-mating, a brand-new movement—if not a whole school —traveling the freeways. Auto-mating is a rolling pickup, far more personal than Lapides's interlude with the green truck.

"Automobiles," wrote Wilson, "are, as everybody knows, sex symbols. Aestheticians and psychologists write scholarly papers on the subject . . . designers hint at some guile in shaping phallic fenders and mammary headlights. We knew that. We didn't know the cars knew."

Auto-mating began for Wilson when a girl in an adjacent lane flashed for him (flashing is the abrupt uncovering of all or part of a human body). He veered to be nearer her exhibitionism. But he was cut off at the pass, or before the pass: "Suddenly another car, a small orange pickup truck, did an 'S' loop in front of me, behind her and round in front of her, the driver gesturing frantically toward the Long Beach South freeway turnoff. She followed."

Wilson was jealous. He felt the callow fellow in the pickup was unworthy of the flasher. He felt he knew them both by what they drove: "Hers was a safe, honest, sensible Volvo with Nordic Minnesota plates . . . the shade of blue I ascribed to her eyes. His was a new, brashly orange Toyota pickup with mag wheels and a university parking bumper sticker."

Wilson began to look for such trouble on the roads. He watched a motorcycle try to form a friendship with a camper, and he was witness when "a plastic-hip stewardess Mustang flirted with an evil-macho-insecure black Stingray." His next participatory event involved another flashing female, when he braked at a signal near Marina Del Rey: "Flash. Great body. A metallic copper Mercedes 350 SL with a Doberman pinscher in the passenger seat. Beyond, a dim impression of long auburn hair and green eyes. A color-coordinated ensemble. Flash. Flash. I smiled, trying for the sincerity of Henry Fonda in *Abe Lincoln in Illinois*. She smiled, conveying the provocative devastation of Jane Fonda in *Barbarella*, whipped her vehicle right in front of mine, adjusted her rearview so I could see her grinning and took off right, sharply, me behind like a modern mechanized caveman crazed with desire."

She led him on a movie-style chase. She laughed just before she deliberately lost him with greater speed and courage: ". . . outmaneuvered and outclassed," admitted Wilson. "I was a fool to think a yellow 1969 Karmann-Ghia (resembling a bumblebee with its black top) could find happiness with a 350 SL with a vanity license plate. The rest of the way home I looked in vain for a nice Love Bug. Maybe it was just too late for a guy with more than 100,000 miles on him."

Wilson finally met an auto-mate on the Hollywood freeway: ". . . five o'clock, suffocatingly hot and smoggy. Old MG sports car. Classy but not snotty like the classic Thunderbird. Yellow with a black top like mine. A few dents suggest some expressiveness and earthiness. We wind up having coffee and enjoying the conversation. 'We'd better have dinner,' I suggest subtly. 'I'd really love to but my life is chaotic right now. I'm fighting with both boyfriends and Saturn is square Cancer which is paralyzing my Venus. Give me your number and I'll call you when it clears up.' "

Wilson, Lapides, and Smith appeared in print just about the time I thought the California affair with the car was almost over, a bad joke we had played on ourselves and then played out. I was wrong, because I didn't consider all the possibilities that appeared with the lowered speed limit and the rising desire to achieve quick connection in the sprawl. Wilson has since heard about the man who drives the freeways in a white Cadillac and tosses weighted pictures of himself into the open windows of cars carrying attractive women. The reverse side of his face has his phone number and an invitation to call.

Only in a culture created by car can love blossom between the lanes. The legendary sexual differences between East and West begin on a roadbed. But I would now like to insist that in matters of cohabiting and commingling, Californians are consistently overrated.

-IX-

Before the Sex, Driven

Some of the American myths are paradoxical. How can we reconcile the notion that the Puritans brought forth a priggish nation with the California reputation for orgies in every orange grove?

The truth is somewhere between the sheets. America does have a heritage of inhibition. And California has grown up furthest from that heritage. California is where topless dancing first jiggled into the national consciousness, in San Francisco in 1964, just about the time Republicans from all over arrived to nominate moral Barry Goldwater for President. California is where the Sexual Freedom League started. California is where most pornographic movies were produced, and where much pornographic print material is manufactured. California is where nude encounter groups raised the level of sensitivity training.

California is where being nude on a public beach has become institutionalized in the seventies, with San Diego marking off a stretch of sand on which it is legal for a person to suit or unsuit himself or herself, where unsuited selves bask together.

But inhibitions and bathing suits are being lost everywhere in the country. I think the distinctions between coasts on matters of work and play are better ways to approach matters of sex.

The people of Boston, New York, and Philadelphia have more of the Puritan ethic in work terms than the people of California. They punch more clocks, keep more regular hours, and preserve more sense of the mandate about earning money for honest labor. Because Easterners are so compulsive about doing their jobs, they are also more relaxed about taking their leisure. Because Westerners are so serious about having time for hedonism, they are almost compulsive about working for pleasure. Californians have a funny tendency to play at work and work at play. New Yorkers work at work, and play only with time left over.

Maybe the point is best made by example, a small true California story about sex that incorporates both California love objects: the car and the soft blonde. Real names will not be used, however, to protect uninnocent people.

Charley Hoxley was newly divorced, nearly fifty, and determined to sample the life of a single swinger. He owned a sports car, rented a furnished apartment, and had a date with Carla, the blonde woman who worked as a receptionist for one of his clients, who also was divorced. She worked in downtown Los Angeles, and so did he. She lived in La Puente. He lived in Westwood, near the UCLA campus. They decided to go to the beach for dinner. Charley's plan was to maneuver her to his apartment on the way home.

The first complication was Carla's. She wanted to go back to La Puente after work so that she could shower, dress, and give the baby-sitter instructions. Would Charley mind picking her up at her apartment? They could then leave in one car.

Charley worked late at the office to kill time. Then he drove seventeen miles to La Puente and picked up Carla, the freshly scrubbed divorcée. Together, they rode to Malibu, Charley insisting that he liked to eat at the ocean when he was with a woman he admired. Charley had driven more than fifty miles when they sat down to dinner.

They had plenty of time to talk. She admired his Corvette. He told her about being a bachelor in a building full of university students. They ate steak, drank Napa Valley wine, and had one brandy after the meal.

On the way back from the beach, Charley casually asked whether Carla might like to see his apartment. He had some good marijuana there; he had recently acquired a taste for it. He had a new stereo system, quadraphonic. He had a collection of Polish circus posters, the current replacement for etchings. She said she liked marijuana.

They shared one joint. Charley really didn't like marijuana, but it was a staple no swinger's household could afford to be without. They went to bed on his kingsize foam-rubber mattress; his landlady forbade waterbeds—too heavy.

128

The second complication was Carla's. She was sleepy, she said. Her sitter could stay over if she called home. Would Charley mind if they slept a little while?

Charley couldn't fall asleep, because Carla snored, but he lay next to her until five A.M. Then they both had to leave. Carla had to be back at La Puente to dress for the working day. Charley drove her there and then waited while Carla showered, changed, and left money for the sitter. At seven-thirty, just in time to catch the regular rush-hour traffic, Charley and Carla rode to downtown Los Angeles and went to their respective offices. Charley, without sleep, wasn't much good at work. He added up the mileage for the night before, and discovered that he'd driven some hundred and fifty miles. But it was worth it, he figured. If they hadn't gone to Malibu, maybe she would have never gone to bed with him.

No standard East Coast sexual animal would find Charley's odyssey worthwhile. That was too much ground to cover, too much time to spend before and after sex, too much energy expended. Business may deserve such drive, but sex should be a chance pleasure.

My friends in the old country on the other coast report no less interest in intimacy than do my California neighbors. Their conversations are no less obsessed with sex. Under their wool hats and camel's-hair coats and rubber galoshes throb the same lusts that move Charley Hoxley.

If California is kinkier, then climate counts. The human body in a warm place makes anatomy a commonplace. The swimsuit, what's left of it, is acceptable street attire. The see-through, look-into, peek-around

129

garment is wearable without chills. The figure exposed to sun is best displayed without strap marks or the stripes of modesty. A tan is an all-year California condition, like a cattle brand proving which cows live on the rich grazing land.

So much everyday skin showing may dull a lascivious appetite or cause a prurient interest to search for dirtier tricks. After all, pornography is an attempt to extend the imagination. Group sex, mate swapping, homosexual intercourse, sodomy, and other once-deviant exercises are strenuous efforts to revive an old act, to make the making of love an ever-popular performance. There are only a few dozen positions the human body can manage—witness the classic erotic art of the Orient, the Near East, and the early Latin American civilizations. A person can do only so much and no more, no matter which culture one comes from or which sports are legitimized.

Casual attire leads to complicated sex. Nudity is not enough in California.

Colder weather clothes the human body in more mystery. Two people coming in from a blizzard on the East Coast may find sufficient warmth in mutual warmth. The regular sex act can be contrast enough to the outside world of freezing wet and fearsome wind.

If California is kinkier, the amusement industry also deserves a few credits under the title. Show business is the business of pleasure, in which entertainment must be worked at, rehearsed, and constantly contrived.

Sex is taken seriously, not casually, by those who produce, direct, and star in it. The lighting must be right. The costume designs have to be accurate. The set

130

needs to complement the contortions. Make-up matters. So do hair style, dialogue, camera angle, and ambient sound. The *Playboy* mentality, in which the meeting of genitals is arranged in the most meticulously architected circumstances, is no less than a motion-picture production reduced to still pictures and translated into a script for unpaid players.

Californians do talk more about sex and their own private parts in the performance of sex. The culture that relies on shrinks and openness and independent movement has to pay lip service to its lack of modesty. The same superficial friendliness that pervades California commerce persists at California cocktail parties. I've heard strangers compare sessions at the analyst's with the same candor with which two Bostonians might trade notes on the collapse of the Red Sox. I've heard women discuss their capacities for orgasm at a canapé table. And I've heard men admit impotence to men and women they hardly know. By California standards, withholding information is more shameful than sexual inadequacy.

None of this conflicts with the privacy passions that govern the West. Saying absolutely anything is absolutely all right, because the speaker knows he or she is protected by whatever real wall surrounds the home or whatever insulation is worn by the individual. Live-and-let-live means each person may be as peculiar as he or she wishes. Admissions of peculiarity do no harm, and they may make conversation livelier.

Since sex is serious business in the West, people become famous for the way they conduct that business or delegate responsibility or manage their intimate affairs. California has sexual celebrities, people known primarily for the way they lead their love lives and not for any other particular talents. Zsa Zsa Gabor, the Hungary I, became a star because of the way she had with men, because of her ability to pretend to be a love object while manipulating escorts, husbands, and hangers-on. Zsa Zsa became a professional actress after her celebrity as an amateur leading lady.

But the symbiotic relationship between making movies and making love is an old California story, as old as the Fatty Arbuckle scandal, the Charlie Chaplin lawsuits, and the Errol Flynn paternity cases. Entertainers have forever been fair game—and unfair game—for gossips, for suitors and lawsuits. The minor-league amusements are also common knowledge: the massage parlors, the swapping bars, and the bottomless pits.

Tourists from the East come to California expecting the worst in sexual oddities, and they search carefully until they find them. Sex businesses are born to meet demand. Just as Californians go to the border towns of Tijuana to relieve their lusts, Easterners come west looking for forbidden pleasures. Sin is a small piece of Mexico. Sin is a thin slice of California. I've made the rounds with tourists, with executives who were content to go from one bottomless bar to another, with writers who wanted to meet the hands that launched a thousand massages, with editors who needed to know whether editorial copy copied life.

They are the visitors who go back east to talk about California as if Carol Doda's silicone chest were the whole spirit of San Francisco and the Classic Cat nude revue the living art in Los Angeles. They quite forget that such attractions essentially cater to the traveling trade, not the natives. The minor-league amusements of California are for out-of-town audiences.

The California sex life that few Easterners know does not bloom in show business. It springs and bounces from aerospace, the bigger bedrock of the Western economy.

Engineers lead more active lives than outsiders suspect. I first came to California as a magazine correspondent with a mandate to specialize in aviation, missiles, and space. I knew almost nothing about apogees, trajectories, and reentries at the time. I also knew almost nothing about the people who made such things happen. I think I expected them to be rigid specialists, subject to abstract absolutes, whose only deviations would be determined by slide rules.

Wrong. Engineers may be exact by day, but almost all the rules slide outside work.

One expert in stress control was almost a marvel at mixing precision with pleasure, at living with paradoxes. He was a proud member of the John Birch Society, convinced that America was being corrupted by Communist influence. He was also a member of a private club in Santa Monica where naked women served lunch to well-dressed men. He was a superbly trained technician. He was an extraordinarily practiced voyeur, pincher, partygoer, and philanderer.

One famous test pilot was a nearly superhuman example to lesser lights in the aerospace field. His warmup for a particularly hazardous mission was wine and women, both taken in massive dosages right up to departure time. He flouted any death fears by flying and by fornicating.

The military had a bearing on the social lives of aerospace. Many of the men maintained their old Air Force habits in civilian work, merely taking off their uniforms while still performing bravely in sex and the sciences.

The pilots were a pervasive influence, even in the commercial airlines. A story once carried me back and forth across the Pacific with several crews from one airline. The social mores of the crews were remarkably similar; the individuals were almost interchangeable.

The typical captain was fifty years old, a former military pilot trained at government expense for a career that would pay about fifty-five thousand dollars a year. The captain loved his family, his land, and large numbers of mechanical gadgets. He tended to be a political conservative.

The co-pilot was in his mid-thirties. The flight engineer was about thirty. The stewardesses were in their twenties, young enough to be the captain's daughters. And, in one sense, a crew functioned as a family. The members stayed in the same hotel, gathered at the swimming pool, and normally dined together. They tended not to wander off by themselves, either to tour or to make new friends.

They usually had a party after dinner, and after the party one of the women usually went to the captain's room. Somehow it seemed important that the captain be a father, social director, and stud. The man charged with the safety of passengers and crew in the air was implicitly charged with planning life on the ground as well. I began to consider the captains as modern versions of the old Western gunfighters. To hold their positions of command, they had to answer every challenge. Now the challenge was more directly connected to the anatomy of manhood. The captain of a high-flying, high-living crew had to be the highest liver of them all. Whether he wanted to or not, the captain was expected to make love as smoothly as he made landings.

Not every aviator lives with his crew. And not every stewardess grounds herself in a harem. But the aviation people of the West are a tight community, remarkably removed from other Californians.

Unlike the other skilled laborers, who are likely to commute from all over the compass rose, they even have their own housing compounds. The descriptions of far-flung California communities of interest don't apply to aerospace and aviation. There is propinquity among the people who fly, or who make flying possible.

High-salaried hands like to live along the coast itself, from Malibu to Palos Verdes in Southern California. Younger crew members and younger technicians clot in the beach cities of Redondo, Hermosa, and Manhattan—especially Manhattan. Manhattan Beach is where stewardesses, flight engineers, space engineers, military consultants, aerospace girls Friday, and systems analysts live in a glorious hodgepodge of apartments and houses. They enjoy casual volleyball, casual leases, and casual sex.

The aerospace crowd was living in communal-like arrangements long before the flower children wandered away from nuclear families into relationships with a lot of new last names. The aerospace free spirits accepted transience and mixed unmarrieds and sex as a healthy exercise twenty years ahead of the hippie movement. The difference was that aviation people also accepted male chauvinism and deplored homosexuality; most of them, remember, had military discipline in their backgrounds.

The modern single swingers are also the nephews and nieces of the crowd that worked in aerospace and launched casual sex as a style in the fifties and sixties. The old California aviation business was where lust was launched without contracts for marriage or money. Part of the aerospace mission was sociological. Old flights of guilt were scrubbed, and many old notions of adultery were aborted.

The women's movement found much of its thesis in antithesis to male-run airplanes and male-bossed aviation industries. Two feminist leaders came to California from the East Coast in 1974 and marveled at the strength of their movement in California. California women, they said, were better organized, better able to understand all the implications of sexism, and better at battling the everyday outrages than their sisters on the opposite shore.

I accept their assessment. I suggest the treatment of women in the movie business and the aviation business raised their consciousness sooner on the West Coast. Even the treatment of women in the student movement of the late sixties created California feminists. During the explosions at Berkeley, San Francisco State, and Santa Barbara, the radical women activists were running the duplicating machines while the men were manning the barricades and the speakers' platforms.

For the primary election of 1974, California voters suddenly saw more than fifty women running for office, nine of them running for statewide office.

California has chapters of each national feminist organization, and a few women's movements all its own. A former art school in Los Angeles has become the Women's Building, housing all-women publishing enterprises, art courses, political outfits, medical counseling, galleries. The lesbian movement is accepted by the women's movement as a parallel response to the way men have behaved.

The homosexual movement is strong at both ends of the state.

San Francisco has long been famous for tolerating what is now called "the gay community." The police and the populace rarely persecuted the homosexual minority.

Los Angeles has lately been less abrasive toward homosexuals. A Gay Community Service Center, the first such establishment in the United States, was opened on Wilshire Boulevard with official support from Los Angeles County, and achieved tax-deductible dignity.

The live-and-let-live ethic, as applied to gays, has caused several politicians to advocate that victimless crimes no longer be prosecuted in California. Some of the gubernatorial candidates took that position. Many local candidates for city attorney have advanced that position, usually in public opposition to the police chiefs who would be their colleagues against crime. When runners for office begin to chase the gay vote, then the gay voters know they have at least become desirable as a power bloc. Politicians obviously think they have more to gain by publicly cultivating gays than by publicly harassing them. New York may have a high concentration of homosexual taxpayers in

Greenwich Village. But Los Angeles has them in Echo Park, Hollywood, Studio City, and all over the map.

More live-and-let-live was applied to another war between the sexes: divorce. At the turn of the decade, California adopted one of the most liberal laws in the country for the end of marriage. Divorce is now called "dissolution," and the only announcement men and women must make to the bureaucracy is that irreconcilable differences exist between them. Anything that two people agree cannot be agreed upon qualifies as an irreconcilable difference, from table manners to toilet habits. The new law was advanced by a state assemblyman who happened to have a concert of interest: The old law punished too many innocent people, and he was one of them. He was one of the early beneficiaries of California's liberalized attitude toward legal dissolution.

The war between the sexes has been more openly declared in California than ever before; statistics for the seventies indicate one divorce for almost every other marriage, a state of constant rupture.

Critics view such shenanigans with alarm. They waggle fingers at the Western toleration for nudity, crudity, and sexuality, blaming a permissive society for allowing itself to destroy so many marriages.

But champions of non-punitive divorce see another side: There wouldn't be so many divorces if marriage weren't still such a popular institution. The divorce figures are weighed down by individuals who have married several times, apparent optimists who still believe the perfect mate is sailing out there somewhere. Californians still expect to be happy, even with each other. The champions ask whether the

138

problem isn't ease of marriage rather than ease of divorce.

I think California optimism is a large cause of both the rupture rate and the remarriage rate. The amusement business, too, is a   factor. Several years ago, before dissolution simplified matters, management whiz Victor Palmieri sat down to discuss divorce with his wife. They were happily married, but they were stunned by the number of Victor's friends who had been wed and then unwed within a decade of college graduation. None of her friends had been divorced. His friends had all grown up on the west side of town, around Beverly Hills, where the movie crowd lived. Her friends grew up east of L.A. in the Pasadena neighborhood, where the older Southern California money was at home.

A similar East-West pattern exists between the coasts. Probably there are no more happy marriages in Boston and Philadelphia than in San Francisco and Los Angeles. But more marriages persist in the Eastern cities. Out of habit. Out of surrounding pressure. Out of fear of not persisting. The Easterners, remember, are the Americans who didn't choose to make the early rupture and run away from home. The Easterners, insists playwright Stanley Price, are more English about remaining married.

Price himself is English. He has worked on both coasts of the United States, most recently in New York and Los Angeles. He brought up the business of divorce when he discovered how many of his old American friends had ended their marriages while he was in London for a few years. The mature Briton, says Price, still remains married in the old way, for better, for worse. The male Briton figures he can't afford to do otherwise. It may not be love of wife or the Anglican Church, but, rather, a fear of having to pay for two households. Austerity remains a fact of English life. And two, however strained their relationship, can still subsist more cheaply than one and one.

Price found the situation on the East Coast about halfway between the situation at home and the rampant-divorce pattern of California. He was most surprised by the Western willingness to admit failure, pay for failure, and begin the mating process all over again.

California optimism, once more. What Californians almost never admit is blame. The geography was what was wrong before they moved out West. The loss of government contracts and the runaway of movie workers was what was wrong when the layoffs came. The relationship—irreconcilable differences—was at fault when the marriage crumbled.

Like children, Californians at work or sex really believe everything will be all right. If not now, then next time. Someone good will kiss it and make it well. Price said the English have no such illusions; that is their survival strength, and their dour weakness. He thought hedonism had much to recommend it, if only his California friends could relax and enjoy it.

A culture that works at pleasure doesn't relax easily. A beautiful, educated divorced California woman once ruined a promising new romance with a handsome, educated, divorced New York man. He tells the story on himself. They were about to go to bed together—her bed—when she asked him, out of courtesy, "What do you like?"

"Whaddya mean?" said the man, honestly confused.

She explained that she wanted to know what sort of sex gave him the most pleasure.

The man wishes he had answered, "Well, what have you got?" Instead, he told her that he didn't know; each time was different from the last, each woman a new experience and, he hoped, a new excitement for him.

She persisted politely, asking questions about oral sex versus genital sex, about positions and placements. She was earnest and eager to be helpful, like a football coach going over all the formations and alignments before the players leave the locker room.

When they finally tumbled into bed, the man could hardly play at all. When she sighed, he figured it was a piece of stage business. When she panted, he figured she might be calling a signal for him. He was never sure how they would line up out of their next huddle. Finally, she passed and he ran. Their affair had been talked to death before it started.

"She had absolute ball control," said the New Yorker, refusing to surrender his football metaphor. "I'd much rather sleep with somebody who hadn't read *The Joy of Sex*, somebody who hadn't decided she could polish her own performance by giving short quizzes before bedtime."

I said earlier that Californians were overrated as sexual animals. This is because they've lost the innocent animal excitements through study, rehearsal, and an attempt at technical mastery. The production number from the movies and the precision analysis from aerospace have combined to reduce simple pleasure rather than enhance it.

And now Californians, who always blame something outside themselves for failure, have found a way to sue for sexual behavior. An attorney named Marvin Wilson has carried two incredible cases to the courts. One involved a San Francisco woman who claimed that a cable-car accident had turned her into a complete nymphomaniac. Another was about a Riverside woman who said that her sex life had steamed up to insufferable temperatures after she had been trapped in a sauna. The San Francisco woman won. Riverside lost. Both cases were conspicuously Californian, in which obsessions about vehicles, beauty, and sex merged to become legal matters. Sex is so open in the West that it retains its monomaniacal quality while losing much of its prurient interest.

The East Coast maintains a sense of mystery about sex, thanks to cold weather, warm clothing, regular hours, and a more developed sense of wariness between members of both sexes. The everyday coldness of human relationships in New York, the low expectations everybody has, heighten the delight of those rare moments when members of each sex manage to couple.

Love, like the landscape, sprawls in California. Love, like the subway, may be deeper and denser in the East. If optimistic Californians insist on having more sex, they also expect more from it. New Yorkers remain realistic: You take what you get and don't ask too many questions.

-X-

California Killer Instincts

Contrasts in sex are no more absorbing than the contrasts in crime.

The older side of the United States has always suffered a deserved reputation for violence. Boston had its strangler. New York had its Mad Bomber. Washington, D.C., has more muggers than bureaucrats. We've already discussed the deadbolt mentality that permeates the East, the fear that rides every subway, and the shielding that surrounds almost every apartment. Such need for self-protection can't be minimized; the ability of law enforcement to offer official protection is severely strained.

The late Claudia Moholy-Nagy, art historian and world sophisticate, told a typical story of rape in New York, with herself as the victim. She came home to her Manhattan apartment late one night. After locking herself in, she discovered she had company. There was a young man in the bedroom, who had almost finished burglarizing the place. Her unexpected arrival turned the simple burglar into an armed robber and rapist.

He pulled a knife on Moholy-Nagy and insisted she share the bed with him. So long as he was there anyway, he might as well enjoy himself and mix pleasure with business. She was too sophisticated and too frightened to fight back.

When it was done, she called the police, describing the incident and the attacker with the kind of exact detail a scholar is trained to note. Reporting rape was rarer in the sixties than it is now, because women were more reluctant to discuss it. Moholy-Nagy, however, considered calling the law an act of duty.

What she couldn't anticipate was the Kafkaesque consequence. Each time the police picked up a young suspect who somewhat resembled her description, they called her to identify the man. The identification calls came at all hours of the night for the next several weeks. At one, two, or three in the morning Moholy-Nagy would be asked to come down to some station house and see whether her attacker was there. Ultimately, this was as painful as the rape had been. And much more prolonged.

Her ordeal was characteristic of East Coast crime: random and routine.

The word for West Coast violence is "ritual."

In the last few years California has become the American capital of mass murder. The Charles Manson collective, charitably called "the Manson Family" is probably the most famous murder combine, because

144

the victims were themselves famous, including movie celebrity Sharon Tate and hair-styling celebrity Jay Sebring. The Mansons were hardly more monstrous, however, than three other mass murderers in the neighborhood of Santa Cruz, California. Nor did the Mansons, in sheer numbers, approach Juan Corona, who was convicted of hiring migrant farm workers and then knocking them off by the dozens after the working day.

Then, in 1974, the Bay Area suddenly sprouted the Symbionese Liberation Army, which abducted Patricia Hearst after gunning down a couple of school administrators. The same year saw the Zebra killings, which put a fresh .38-caliber panic between black-white relations.

A *Harper's* writer, Barry Farrell, moved to California and tried to find a conspiracy theory that would lend logic to mass murders of the West, from the assassination of Robert Kennedy to the Manson butchery. The irresistible temptation is to look for mystic connections in California. After all, this was the state that had produced more funny cults than fine culture. This is where kookiness is next to Godliness. And Farrell was able to see a temporal thread between executions in the modern West; when one set of mass murders ended, another series sprang up.

But no other leads led to any demonstrable conclusions. In fact, the evidence is otherwise. The Symbionese crowd claimed political inspiration. The Zebras were reverse racists. The Mansons came out of the dregs of the drug subculture. The killers of Santa Cruz were single agents, however insane. The Zodiak murderer of the San Francisco area, a creature who is apparently still at large but no longer active, preyed on young couples in lonely lovers' lanes.

The difference between hideous crime on the two coasts is essentially everyday terror in the East versus orchestrated barbarism in the West. Boston's strangler and New York's Bomber turn out to be rule-proving exceptions to the patternless violence that saturates the Eastern streets. Both of them would have been more at home in California, where mass murder seems to have ritualistic meanings. Just as sex may be more happenstance in the East, so is brutality. Brutality in the West has a terrible quality of being rehearsed, perfected, and performed—each mass murderer with his or her own act to top the acts that happened earlier.

Crime is still not a constant scare in California. People walk the streets at night. People still leave cars unlocked. Some people even leave their homes open, unafraid of brutes and burglars. Each time we visit the East we are astonished by the printed warnings in hotel rooms, the elaborate guarding of apartment houses, and the stories told by residents. The East, not the West, sits in a series of stockades, armed against the constant threat of invasion by hostile outsiders.

Crime among middle-class teen-agers, a hybrid aberration, is probably more common in the West, where young people have more mobility and more complaints. Some of the Western teen-agers who don't run away escape instead by living outside the law.

California writer Mike McFadden found an almost archetypical example for *New Times* magazine in Irvine, California. The largest drug net in the history of the West involved one hundred officers of the law arresting one hundred drug users and drug traders in early 1974. Most of the traffickers in narcotics were teen-agers, the depressed children of upper-middle affluence.

The accused were also the unplanned spoils of a planned community. Irvine is in Orange County, between San Diego and Los Angeles. It is a new town, carved almost overnight out of the old Irvine Ranch, which was the largest hunk of undeveloped livable land in Southern California until the 1960s. Newport Beach and Laguna Beach, Irvine neighbors, are enclaves of old wealth. The new University of California at Irvine has brought a few freer spirts to the area, but even the campus operates with a sense of Orange County constraint.

The Irvine developers could make large promises to potential residents of the new town. The explicit inducements were suburban, with splashes of land-use controls tossed in for modern measure: "In these new villages," said an Irvine Company sales pitch, "life is more peaceful and fulfilling than in a community that does not have these planning advantages." These "planning advantages" were dead-end streets and bike trails and architectural harmonies. The implicit inducements were also historic-suburban: no gang fights in the schools, no downtown densities, no dramatic injection of economic or ethnic diversity.

McFadden found a teen-ager who described Irvine this way: "The place is so homogenized, middle class and blah, the kids really have to hunt for something exciting to do."

Something exciting for some of them to do was simple burglary. A fifteen-year-old found that the community lent itself to casing: "You can get the floor plan of any house you want from the sales office." McFadden also quoted a kid on the ease with which a young criminal could make his escape—over the rooftops and trails and lovingly landscaped hillocks of the neighborhoods. It was easier to elude the law in Irvine than in crowded downtowns.

Something exciting for others was dope, as a way to elude boredom. "It's an escape from the bullshit at home," claimed one teen-ager, "there's an identification—it's status to dope—and it's an easy way to get into sex."

The various law enforcers spent three months gathering evidence against the young masterminds. It wasn't difficult. These were softened criminals. A reporter who covered the story on a daily basis said, "It was like watching a game of cops and robbers where the cops were real and the robbers pretend."

One sixteen-year-old dealer in methamphetamines was charged with selling speed to an undercover official and, after his arrest, admitted: "I guess I really knew he was a narc, but it really didn't matter. He was a cool guy, and when he asked me if I could get him some whites, I said yes, as much as he wanted. He looked like a Hell's Angel, and I wanted him to like me."

The need for approval among the young Irvine dopers was a fairly exact inversion of their parents' need to be accepted, approved, and adjusted in the new community. The adults appeared powerless in terms of

148

stopping the drug situation at home before the officers arrived. McFadden wrote about a raid on one particular pad in Irvine to which the youngsters had gone to cure their blahs. As the police dragged them outside and plopped them into a paddywagon, a group of adult neighbors stood on the sidewalk and cheered. And one man confessed to the cops, "I don't like to see this, but what the hell took you guys so long?"

The developers couldn't explain how something so chaotic could happen in such a nice neighborhood. An executive from the Irvine Company said, "All the kids want to talk street talk and be tough. The trouble is, we don't have any streets—just culs-de-sac, lanes, and parkways. We tried to order these communities so they worked, but maybe there are things in this society you just can't order."

Maybe. In this unhappy case of arrested development are so many broken aspects of the California dream: the notion that there's always room to run; the idea that family structure can be strengthened by residential structure; the belief that crime is committed by undesirables who live in undesirable neighborhoods.

Again, Californians who can afford to insulate themselves from contemporary urban woes turn out to be woefully unequipped to deal with woe on their own doorsteps.

My mail from Irvine is full of letters from outraged parents who blame other parents for what happened, who say permissiveness is the rotten root of Irvine's troubles, who insist the leashes are too long to control family strays. The contradictions in California conservatism are all there. These are the same people who don't like government, taxes, managed economies, or any form of social subsidy to the poor. They want to be left alone, without interference from bureaucratic big brothers. However, they also want strict enforcement for everyone else. They want controls, restraints, and riot acts applied by the law so they can enjoy their own liberty.

By statewide initiative, Californians voted for a return to capital punishment during the seventies. The citizens who want government removed from their lives also want government to remove those other lives that are seen to be dangerous.

The police agencies of California tend to be more absolute and more honest than their Eastern counterparts. Graft and corruption are more common to the East Coast, because a tolerance for cynicism lives there. So does tolerance for error and weakness. Weakness, like personal blame, is what's not admitted to in the West. Brutality in the name of the law is more acceptable to most Californians than bending of the law.

We are a punitive people, I think, because we have never really learned how to be parents. And so we say we know what's best for other people, unable to be sure what's best for ourselves.

One other kind of crime seems uniquely at home in California: big business fraud. Specks of the Gold Rush still cling to Western newcomers, those who come to seek their fortunes by their own efforts and those who come to filch their fortunes by investing other people's efforts.

150

The Great Wall Street Scandal, a book by Raymond Dirks and Leonard Gross, is a misplaced title. The most monstrous swindle of modern America, in which more than one hundred million dollars' worth of phony assets were created by computer, didn't happen on Wall Street at all. The scandal was born, raised, and ripened in the Los Angeles headquarters of Equity Funding Corporation of America—a giant diversified financial company that started with ten thousand dollars in 1960 and claimed to manage one billion dollars when it burst in 1973. No other firm became so big so fast anywhere.

Nowhere but in Los Angeles would Equity's astonishing apparent growth have been accepted so easily as a matter of fact. When a federal grand jury indicted Equity employees in 1973, no fewer than twenty hirelings were involved on no less than one hundred five counts of fraud and conspiracy.

Dirks and Gross begin their account with a description of Equity Funding's headquarters and President Stanley Goldblum: "His office was a summit of sorts. It stood in the choicest corner of the highest floor of the handsomest building in the country's most sumptuous financial complex." In that space Stanley Goldblum reserved thirty feet by twenty-five feet for himself, complete with a fake fireplace.

Such opulence, such artifice, came almost naturally to Century City. Century City broke ground in the late 1950s on the western side of the Beverly Hills border, on land that used to belong to Twentieth Century–Fox. Movies were made there when sound stages kept the business indoors and near Hollywood. But Fox shrank, and Alcoa picked up the real-estate pieces to build a subcity of Los Angeles that would dwarf the landlocked island of Beverly Hills.

Century City has high-rise office buildings, a fancy crescent-shaped hotel, a major commercial shopping center, and expensive condominium apartments. It also has dozens of financial firms which rushed in to capitalize on the newest plush address with the newest plush carpet. The developers themselves have admitted that Century City attracted fast-buck boys who trade on fancy façades.

After the poisoned air came out of the Equity balloon, a young writer for *Forbes* magazine called the project "Century Silly," in honor of the scandal and the other money-management outfits who made quick livings jerry-building tax shelters or syndicates. The *Forbes* man was slightly unfair. Reputable financial companies occupy Century City still. Some of them now use Los Angeles as their post-office address, preferring to ignore the plush name that Equity stained. But silly fleecing and sophisticated fleecing is an old Southern California story. The get-rich greed in the law-abiding community is what allows the greed in the crooked community to flourish with so few questions raised.

When the honest Wall Street market is good, the dishonest operators enjoy exceptional success. When the market is down, the corrupters suffer, because greedy optimism is tempered everywhere. So Century City, after Equity, was slightly depressed by scandal and by a downturn on faraway Wall Street. Charles Rosenberg, a young broker who used to do honest business in a building across the street from Equity, once said it was a good thing the new high-rises were all air-conditioned. It wasn't the comfort of cool he appreciated so much as the consequent sealing of the windows. You can't open the windows of Century City, and so you can't jump out of them after you've cheated or been cheated.

-XI-

West of the White House

Eastern politics are traditionally pulled by political machines.

California politics have almost always been hauled by political animals, a strange assortment of maverick creatures who tugged right and left and never attended obedience school in either party.

One of the explanations for California's peculiar political processes is the nature of a refugee state. Only two of the last six governors, for instance, have been born in California. More than half of the more than twenty million people have come from somewhere else.

Gladwyn Hill covered California politics for *The New York Times* for decades and claimed the state was a cross section of the whole United States, with a proportionate number of people from everywhere. He pointed out California's almost uncanny ability to mirror the national mandate: Only twice in the twentieth century did the state not vote for the winning Presidential candidate, and both misses were by hairline margins. One of the misses was when native son Richard Nixon lost to John Kennedy in 1960. And University of California political scientist Eugene Lee saw another statistical significance in that election; the Berkeley professor looked at Nixon's margin of 35,600 votes and realized that 86,000 Californians had gone to the polls but refused to pick a President that year. More than twice as many voters refused to choose between Nixon and Kennedy as opted to give Nixon his narrow margin.

Conventional California wisdom says party registration means almost nothing in terms of particular election returns. Conventional wisdom is correct for a change. California is Democratic by a better than five-to-four margin, but California began the seventies by reelecting conservative Republican Ronald Reagan and reendorsing Richard Nixon for the White House.

Modoc County is the state's most reliable barometer, a land-large, population-tiny square of territory at the most northeastern corner of California. As Modoc, with its fewer than five thousand registered voters, has gone, so has the state.

The nearly unanimous California elections can be claimed by Republicans. In 1928 Hiram Johnson won all counties on his way to the governorship. So did Earl Warren in 1950. Until 1959, cross-filing was allowed in California, meaning that a candidate for office could compete in as many primaries as there were parties. Warren could appear as both a Democrat and a

Republican in 1950, winning the endorsement of each to guarantee his success in the final election.

Hill writes about the first Democratic rally, in 1849, at which the delegates issued a self-defeating declaration: "Partyism for the sake of party, we totally reject." Such loyalty to lack of loyalty has characterized California ever since.

Where political blocs rub up against one another and shift, splinter groups constantly appear. California had the People's Independent Party in 1873, declaring party loyalty to be "that tyrannical rule which degrades the citizen and sinks him to the servile partisan, rendering him the helpless tool of selfish wire-pullers and caucus-manipulators."

The 1870s were also blessed in the West with a Workingmen's Party that didn't merely grind axes, but carried them in order to persuade voters.

Upton Sinclair led the left during the 1930s and ran for governor. The John Birchers formed a bastion for the right in the 1960s and made California safe for the nomination of Barry Goldwater.

Probably only in California could a socialist (Gaylord Wilshire) become the ultimate capitalist and land developer; Los Angeles' fanciest boulevard was named after him.

The struggles in the East are usually between the rural vote, upstate, and the urban vote, downstate. California's picture is not nearly so clear. Upstate, including the city of San Francisco, generally votes left of downstate, embracing Los Angeles. Some of the heaviest Republican concentrations are around the megalopolis of Los Angeles, in Orange and Riverside Counties. Some of the most consistently Democratic returns have come from the rural areas in Shasta and Plumas Counties, well north of San Francisco.

The state is nearly one thousand miles long, an extraordinary bandwagon for any political animal to attempt hitching to; the distance between San Francisco and Los Angeles, two cities whose citizens have different selfish needs, is almost five hundred miles.

Name identification is what California seekers of statewide office claim is the most necessary and most elusive ingredient of any campaign.

Name identification has caused some rich comedy in recent elections. During the last two gubernatorial years there have been the Flournoys on the Republican primary ballet. One was Houston Flournoy. The other was James Flournoy. Houston had been a college professor, an assemblyman, and the state controller. James had been a minor party functionary. In 1970 Houston was running for reelection as controller. James was running for secretary of state. Houston is white. James is black. Houston won the primary and general election. James won the primary and lost the general election.

In 1974, both of them were back. Houston, now a household name, was running for governor to replace Ronald Reagan. James, still "the other Flournoy," was running for Houston's old job as controller. One of James Flournoy's Republican opponents, Assemblyman William Bagley, was furious. Bagley charged James with name-bagging—entering a race for an office only because the voters might confuse him with the outgoing officeholder. Houston Flournoy won his primary battle and wound up in the finals against Edmund G. Brown, Jr., the outgoing secretary of state, who had beaten—guess who?—James Flournoy in the finals of 1970. James Flournoy lost his primary battle.

If two Flournoys looked better than one, the Democratic game of the name has been no less interesting lately. The Edmund G. Brown, Jr., who triumphed over James Flournoy for secretary of state in 1970, to become the only state-level elected official from the Democratic Party during Reagan's second term, was the son of the Edmund G. "Pat" Brown who was governor from 1958 to 1966.

Edmund Brown, Sr., had a roller-coaster career of his own. The liberals loved him when he first became governor. He helped the causes of higher education; he helped advance the dignity of minority groups. The liberals were furious at him in 1960 for finally executing Caryl Chessman, a book-writing kidnapper and robber who lived on death row for twelve years.

Brown, Sr., was up again for the election of 1962, when he faced Richard Nixon as his opponent for governor. Californians forgive fast. Now Pat Brown was hailed as the executive who had made the Feather River Project a reality and assured plentiful northern waters for the parched part of the state down south.

In 1962, Richard Nixon was going down. He had lost the presidency to upstart John Kennedy. He was a former vice-president of the United States coming home to be governor of California. A step lower, for sure, but one that he would adjust to as a professional. Being governor was better than being out of work.

In retrospect, the results are almost incredible. They were even fairly startling at the time. Nixon, the national figure who had come within a chinwhisker of the White House, lost to the incumbent who could hardly hold his own statewide party together at the previous national convention. Nixon, the trim, lost to Brown, the paunchy. Nixon, the experienced debater, lost to Brown, the folksy blusterer. All attentive Americans will remember that Richard Nixon took the 1962 defeat as his own political death sentence. That was the year he made his valedictory against the press, blaming the media for his unfortunate demise and sarcastically assuring them they wouldn't have Nixon to kick around any more.

It was a memorable night in the Beverly Hills Hotel. Dick snarled. Pat cried. And dozens of reporters thought they had indeed seen the last of the candidate who had begun his career by baiting Reds and would end it by baiting journalists.

But Californians are indeed forgiving. And they have short memories. With their help, Pat Brown was able to survive the Chessman fiasco, and Richard Nixon would rise again to run for highest office. Turn the country around : Could a man who couldn't be elected governor of New York rise to be president six years later, handily winning his own home state along the way? I think not. But New York, as I'll insist later, finally did more for Richard Nixon than California did.

It was no accident, I think, that Richard Nixon moved to New York and practiced law while rebuilding his strength for the great American comeback. Party loyalty was and is important in New York. Past favors are more easily paid back in the East, where memories tend to be longer and forgiveness is not proffered so fast.

Pat Brown's roller coaster, meanwhile, started a

159

downhill run. He could beat moderately conservative Richard Nixon in 1962, but he couldn't come close to catching confirmed conservative Ronald Reagan in 1966. Reagan, of course, had name identification of a special kind, which will be considered a few paragraphs from here. But the same Brown who had triumphed over a congressman–senator–vice-president wound up losing to a man who previously had never been elected anything.

The household name of Brown was cruelly reduced to the plumbed depths of California residences. One of the campaign bumper strips of the time read, IF IT'S BROWN, FLUSH IT—probably the most indelicate mandate of an indelicate region.

But a Brown, Edmund, Jr., was back by 1970 and moving up. The race for secretary of state that year was a California classic, because two relatively unknown candidates with impressive borrowed name identification confronted each other: James Flournoy, the unrelated Flournoy, versus Edmund G. Brown, the junior Brown. Junior—Gerry to his friends—won easily. After all, a candidate confused with a former governor should do better than a candidate confused with a controller.

The confusion was quite real. California is so big that ignorance of the lawmakers is a legitimate excuse. Familiarity breeds more comfort than contempt.

The price of distance is politically dear in the West, especially applied to name identification. One of the candidates in the Democratic primary for the same gubernatorial nomination of 1974 was Congressman Jerome Waldie—another Jerry to his friends. Waldie had been a successful state assemblyman, but that had been in the sixties, and California memories, remember, are short. His several terms as member of the House would not help him hold statewide identification.

First of all, California has more congressmen than any other state. And a representative from the East Bay area of Antioch is not going to get as much media attention as the representatives from San Francisco and Los Angeles. Waldie suffered for having left Sacramento for the larger legislature in Washington, D.C., as strange as that may seem to Eastern readers.

When politicians graduate from statehouses in Pennsylvania, New Jersey, or Massachusetts to Washington, D.C., they can operate as big fish in both ponds, the small old one and the big new one. They can commute to their constituencies continuously, shuttling back and forth from home district to Capitol Hill. They can play with local pork barrels and national policy at the same time, remaining close to the state party and keeping in personal touch with the local media.

But when a Californian goes off to Congress, he is almost lost to his constituency for two years. Even Alphonzo Bell, the rare commuter who comes home to Coldwater Canyon every weekend, has less contact with his district than lower officeholders, and hardly any statewide recognition.

So when Jerry Waldie went up against a field of other serious Democrats trying to be governor, he had a serious handicap from the start. Gerry Brown held statewide office, in addition to his father's coattails. Bob Moretti had statewide identity, because he had become Speaker of the same Assembly Waldie had worked for before Waldie became a national figure. Joseph Alioto was mayor of San Francisco, a job that guarantees recognition second only to sourdough bread.

Waldie ran behind these three in all the early polls. He appeared with the also rans in these polls: with a distinguished Bay Area businessman, William Matson Roth; with a prominent attorney, Herb Hafif; with a Los Angeles County supervisor, Baxter Ward. Nothing he did raised him to real contention. Not a walking tour of the state, a tactic that helped Dan Walker become governor of Illinois. Not membership on the House Judiciary Committee, a happy accident of timing that allowed him to talk with some authority on the impeachability of Richard Nixon. And not, most of all, his considerable credentials as the candidate who knew California from a national perspective.

Outside inner political circles, nobody knew who Jerry Waldie was. What he needed more than a seat in Washington was a father who had been in politics or, failing that, another Waldie who had walked in Sacramento during the years he was away.

But when proper Philadelphians think of chaotic California politics, they don't concern themselves with distance and the difficulty of trying to talk on platforms that will impress people from the Forty-second Parallel approaching Oregon to below the Thirty-Third Parallel at the Mexican border.

Show business is what seems to them so peculiar about the way the West is won. They marveled at George Murphy in the sixties. George Murphy, the man who once danced with Shirley Temple and soft-shoed his way across the silver screen, ran for the Senate. And he was elected, over the stout body of Pierre Salinger, who was the appointed incumbent and former press secretary for John Kennedy.

They marveled at Shirley Temple Black, who once danced with George Murphy, when she started running for the House of Representatives. Shirley, a conservative, came close in the Republican primary, but she couldn't overcome the sexism still rampant in the late sixties.

They marveled most of all at Ronald Reagan, the star who hardly danced with anybody but was a movie man on horseback, when he became governor in 1966. The East was unprepared for stardom so easily transferred: from the host of *Death Valley Days* on television to the boss of the most populous state in the country. The left-liberals in the East were left wondering whether a treat Reagen as a hilarious amusement, a miscat cowboy, or a potential threat to more conventional political animals. The simplest response was to blame California for producing one of its kookiest performances yet, to assume that Ronald Reagan was merely going to mouth the lines for an adolescent state that never had known what it wanted to be when it grew up.

One of the plot twists since Reagan's first election has been the man's strength in office. Whatever his tendencies to be a troglodyte in matters of social welfare, Reagan must be taken seriously. He is an intelligent man. He is an extraordinarily quick study, better briefed for campaign questions than any other officeholder in the West. And he is personally honest.

Jeremy Larner once described Reagan for

Harper's as the most intelligent shallow man he'd ever met. The judgment carries truth and cruelty. Reagan is not profound; he probably approaches true-believer status in his loyalty to a political philosophy. Both his friends and enemies remind California audiences that Reagan was a Democrat in his earlier days, was once the president of the Screen Actors Guild and thereby once a union man. His switch to conservatism came fairly late in his complicated career. But once Reagan was committed, he embraced conservatism with all the adamancy of a convert.

I have never seen a more consummate campaigner for any office anywhere. And I say that as a warning to any East Coast thinkers who would not consider Ronald Reagan seriously as a presidential candidate for 1976. Only the Nixon resignation leading to the Ford ascension makes Reagan's chances bleak.

Let me be specific. I traveled with Reagan down the belly of California in the gubernatorial race of 1970. One day the governor was going from Sacramento to Fresno through the rich San Joaquin Valley, talking to growers and fieldworkers alike. The Valley is rich, because its produce feeds the state and the nation. The growers do extremely well. Some of the wealthiest and most heavily subsidized agribusinesses in America grow right around Fresno. California's annual harvest from farming is almost eight billion dollars, more money than the Michigan auto industry brings in each model year. But the farmworkers themselves, whether organized by Cesar Chavez's union or by the Teamsters, are poor. They are the modern migrants, mostly Mexican, who come and go with the crops. They spend the spring in Coachella

Valley, in Southern California, and follow the lettuce and grapes into summer as they mature above Bakersfield. Workers live in temporary housing. They use their children as field hands in order to eke out piecework livings at the poverty level. They have no job security against the acts of God or growers.

When Reagan came to talk to such laborers at the Merced County Fair, I expected him to be hooted off the platform. The Republican Party traditionally welcomes stoop labor without improving the lives of families who perform it. The Reagan administration has consistently been kinder to owners than to pickers. Reagan's 1970 opponent, Jess Unruh, came from a poor farm family himself; he was a transplanted Texan who could honestly claim identification with the miseries of migrant life. But Unruh never had such sweet, ripe audiences in the Valley.

The governor was a smash in Merced that day. The brown faces in front of him softened into smiles. The workers applauded. Reagan didn't say much, and he avoided labor issues with the care of a man wearing new boots in a field full of fertilizer. He simply congratulated the county for its agricultural bounty. He talked about the magnificent contribution to the nourishment of America made by all the people who worked the area.

When these sun-creased faces folded into admiration, I decided they had been starstruck. A hero on screen and television had come to their county and made a personal appearance. The political purpose was less important than the attractive presence.

Reagan spoke without notes, without pomp, and without partisanship. He answered questions from the audience without once causing controversy. The only stand he took was being there. And they loved him.

That was the day I decided show business is superb training for politics. It has obvious advantages for candidates who have to squeeze their messages through a tube. It has other advantages for candidates who must meet the people without embarrassment or condescension. Ronald Reagan has the grace of having given autographs, having learned how to look directly at people, how to shake hands with manly strength.

This is performance, extremely persuasive performance. The aloof likes of a Nixon or a Eugene McCarthy can't compare with Reagan's ability to handle the role of leader, leading man, and fast friend. Since all campaigning is performance, there's no diminishing Reagan on the grounds that he is only acting or reading his lines well. He is simply a better political actor than other Californians—and one of the reasons he gives a good reading is that he believes in the part.

Scandals have touched the Reagan administration without tainting the governor. Money has been mishandled. Bribery has been proved. His lieutenant governor, Ed Reinecke, hand-picked by Reagan himself in 1966, has been convicted in the wake of Watergate for lying about the ITT matter. The Watergate overflow lapped around Sacramento, but Ronald Reagan never got wet. Even Reagan's staunchest enemies have never accused the governor of personal corruption. There was a proved charge that he paid no state income tax one year despite his comfortable salary, his real-estate holdings, and his investments.

But Reagan could show that he only took advantage of his legal loopholes, honestly accounting for the tax shelters that protected him.

Now the question becomes whether this western hero can ever turn himself into a national leading man. The early polls (before Nixon's departure) for the nomination of 1976 had Gerald Ford and Ronald Reagan at the top of the Republican pile. And my East Coast old friends were laughing. They still find it inconceivable that a rerun cowboy could ride his way into the White House.

The East could learn more by admitting the downright appeal of this upright Californian than by continually misinterpreting the vague social movements in the West.

The Eastern sages might see the world differently if they had watched what happened in Merced, or if they merely stopped believing their own tastes were so transferable.

In 1974 critics and political scientists on both coasts were theorizing on what would happen after Watergate was done with. The possibilities, said several, included a violent wrench toward the left and an opposite stampede to the right. If the country turned left, it would be from loss of faith in present institutions as well as present leaders. If America went right, the loss of faith might seem less complete, meaning the institutions are better than the people operating them. That's a seductive argument, of course: Save the Constitution but tighten the screws. Wheeling to the right would have the appearance of preserving a government of laws while improving the people. The danger, less apparent, would be the imposition of police-state restrictions on civil rights in the name of absolute morality.

Prize-winning historian Page Smith, bred in the East and living in California, thinks the tilt rightward is more likely than the slant left. If that happens, Ronald Reagan, man of purity and certainty, may yet emerge as the perfect proponent of the next morality.

I do agree that the unhumble beginning of Reagan's political career could not have happened in the East. The man walked out of the studios and into the hearts of his statewide constituents without ever pausing to occupy lower office. Reagan's previous experience on political platforms was limited to national tours in behalf of business sponsor General Electric and campaign sponsor Republican Party. He was superb among the cigar set, delivering pungent pep talks to the well-do-do in large hotel ballrooms. Such one-nighters allowed him to polish his delivery without risk, because he wasn't running for anything.

These were the nights when Reagan learned to provoke laughter. He was never much of a light comedian in the movies, but he turned into a needle-sharp satirist of the left when he toured the banquet circuit. Humor helped him immensely during the campaign of 1970. When opponent Jess Unruh started visiting Republican fat cats at their homes in order to attract media attention, Reagan didn't pretend outrage at the invasions of privacy. He joked instead about Unruh's house calls and how undignified it was for a would-be governor to go around like a mad doctor offering absurd prescriptions to people who weren't sick.

168

Reagan, the media-made man, has fared better than some other California performers. No account of Western political phenomena should omit Sam Yorty, the three-term mayor of Los Angeles. Mayor Sam began as a refugee from Nebraska who sometimes played saxophone in public. He too went through a couple of reincarnations during his career in government. Yorty was a liberal congressman at one time. He was a conservative congressman at another time. He was a maverick mayor during his heydays of the sixties, nominally a Democrat but ideologically almost nowhere. He supported Richard Nixon for President in 1968, and announced he was available for a cabinet post in return.

When Yorty was running the third largest city in the country, he was also running for other offices. During his twelve years at City Hall, Sam ran for governor, U.S. Senator, and President of the United States. It was as if he couldn't pass up an election. The run for the Presidency was probably his last straw vote against the wind. In 1972, Yorty went to the Democratic convention with a few friends and a little bizarre support from a conservative New Hampshire newspaper publisher. He was welcomed as a sort of a joke on the East Coast, but he was also moonlighting with the media at the time. A Los Angeles radio station was using Yorty as political commentator as well as Presidential candidate.

Sam, his reedy delivery up in his nasal passages, was no stranger to electronic-news amusement. He had his own Sam Yorty show on one of the independent television channels during his second term in the mayor's office. The Yorty program was significantly

169

different from the show simultaneously put on by John Lindsay in New York. Then-mayor Lindsay appeared in his official guise as city executive, using the exposure to inform the citizens. If Lindsay also used the time to advance his own political career, he was nonetheless earnest about being on television for substance.

The Sam show, in contrast, treated municipal matters quite lightly. The mayor appeared as a kind of minor-league Johnny Carson: affable, chatty, showbizzy. In fact, show-business celebrities were part of the regular order of interviews, and Sam treated them with the deference of foreign dignitaries. Sam, the former sax player, was obviously rehearsing a new act in case one of his multiple candidacies failed to come through.

John Lindsay appeared out of the goodness or badness of his elected heart.

Sam Yorty was paid for his appearances as Los Angeles's highest host. And although many Southern Californians objected to seeing the mayor make money on commercial television, the program continued until its natural death by ratings.

After Yorty was finally voted out of the mayor's office in 1973, he once again turned to the media for nourishment, taking a radio job as morning talk-show host to the telephoning masses. By the summer of '74, Yorty was the darling of the aging right, and his callers invariably called him "Mayor Sam."

One of the funnier aspects of Yorty's split mayor-media personality was his rather constant war with the press. They were out to get him, the mayor claimed, especially the Los Angeles *Times* and the

170

local network television stations. But he was so successful at blurring the old boundaries between running things and reporting things that several other
only-in-California candidates have come along in his
footsteps.

Baxter Ward was an ABC anchorman in Los
Angeles, the butt of an old joke about the way different
stations approached the catastrophes of the day.
Whereas the local CBS man was accused of reading the
news and KTTV was charged with slanting the news,
KABC was said to ignore the news. Ward was an ag-
gressive newscaster, with more human interest than
issue interest. He was one of Yorty's many opponents
for mayor in the 1969 campaign. Then, in 1972, Ward
managed to run a tired L.A. county supervisor out of
office. In 1974, Ward turned Democrat to launch a
losing campaign in the gubernatorial primary.

Meanwhile, other men from the media were
leaving the safety of observation posts for the risk of
political careers. And at about the time Ward declared
for the Democrats, Sam Yorty finally made his move to
the Republican Party.

In California it becomes ever more difficult to tell
the players from the pundits, to distinguish where
show busines ends and statesmanship begins. That
seems healthy to most of us, who have never really
seen a smooth political machine. But I know it looks
like a yahoo circus from the East, where political
giants such as Abraham Beame work their way up
through the ranks for decades before ever assuming
control of a major city.

California not only tolerates inexperience, it tends
to encourage it. There were eighteen candidates for

governor in 1974 on the Democratic side alone. The professional credentials those eighteen chose to put beneath their names on the ballet are a fair cross section of anything goes—or anyone goes. There was Raymond Chote, a philosopher. There was Josephum Ramos, a warehouseman. There was George Henry Wagner, a construction truck driver. There was Joseph Brouillete, who was content to have nothing listed under his name as a qualification. And there was Eileen Anderson, a singer.

Eileen Anderson deserves more than simply "singer," and she's worth a little more than a tag-end sentence to finish a paragraph. Eileen Anderson may be the quintessential combination of show business, exhibitionism, and innocence in one California candidate. Like Yorty, Anderson has appeared on a bunch of primary ballots over the years. Unlike anybody else, she began her public career in a bathing suit in a courtroom. Eileen Anderson was claiming damages in an accident, and acting as her own counsel. She wanted to show bruises, and so she wore a green swimsuit to her historic damage suit, thereby attracting immediate media attention and a dollop of fame. That was at the turn of the sixties, long before nude movies and naked streakers; even in California, a body in a bathing suit was a rarity in the courtroom.

But her suit was not enough. She ran for mayor many times, and sang her praises to the people, a capella—without any accompaniment or many supporters. Losing on each occasion, Eileen Anderson tried to perform the Hollywood trick of failing upward, and ran for governor. She sang her campaign again, using some of the same material she had developed in the late sixties. Alas, she lost again. There are signs that the once-voluptuous Anderson candidacy is sagging, and she may have to move East, where experience is a greater credential than gall.

Voting is itself a difficult act to follow in California. My favorite approach to the unusual ordeal is a true story of the middle sixties, before we even had computer punch cards in the West. A man named Albert M. Nickleby burst a blood vessel within the privacy of a polling place. The evidence appeared in the official insurance claim filed with the county registrar by the owner of the home in La Mirada where it all occurred: "While Albert M. Nickleby, the last voter of the day, stood in the voting booth, a blood vessel in the lower portion of his neck ruptured and the loss of a great deal of blood resulted. The carpeting on which he stood became blood-soaked and subsequently required the services of a professional rug cleaning service to remove the stain."

In one sense, Nickleby bled to save us all. The day he burst we were still trying to vote under primitive physical conditions. The booths were smaller than telephone booths. The writing surface was a belly-high slat of wood no deeper than a rowboat seat. The marker was a rubber stamp about one-third the length of a pencil, always inky and gummy from previous voters. The ballot on Nickleby's big day was almost two feet long and sixteen and a half inches wide— much too large for the wood slat. And if the meticulous voter brought a sample ballet to the polling place, then he or she had two paper banners too big for the table.

The psychological conditions were worse. That was the year Nickleby faced forty-eight choices: nine statewide offices; one congressional candidate; fourteen judgeships; seventeen state measures, including fifteen constitutional amendments; four county questions, two school-tax measures, and one city-charter amendment to resolve. The Western heritage to reform led to the bloated ballet, in which dozens of decisions were passed along to the people for resolution—many of them questions that could have been decided by the legislature.

Now we have computer cards in California, and the physical circumstances have improved. But the psychological demands are still enough to burst a blood vessel. My primary ballot for 1974 offered forty-three choices: eight statewide offices; one U.S. Senator and one Congressman; two state legislators; seven members of the county committee in the party of my choice; seven judges, a sheriff; an assessor; a county supervisor; nine state measures; two city measures; two school-district measures; and one water-district bond issue.

The California way of helping the burdened voter make up his or her mind is with brochures. I received several prior to election day. One was a fifty-five-page pamphlet from the State explaining nine measures in small type and legal language. Another was a twelve-page submission by the school district, folded like a poster. The County held itself to two pages. But the city issued a fourteen-pager with some of the worst writing of the season, ending in this single sentence:

Should the New System, prior to or during the fiscal year 1967–1968, have insufficient funds in its New System Service Pension Fund or

in its New System General Pension Fund, or in
both, to pay pensions granted pursuant to this
Article or to pay the administrative expenses of
the System and of the Fire and Police Pension
System provided by Article XVII of this Charter,
then the Council shall appropriate sufficient
moneys therefor to the New System General Pension Fund as a loan and such loan shall be repaid
from the first available moneys in said fund.

The Metropolitian Water District poured in four
pages more. And eleven candidates paid for the privilege of placing statements of their qualifications in
one of the mailing packets.

California has a state law allowing us ten minutes
to make all these choices in the booth. No sane citizen
can decide so much in so little time. So a citizen who
cares has to study all those pamphlets before election
day and know the choices before going into the polling
place. The work is hard.

Harry Ashmore of the Center for the Study of
Democratic Institutions at Santa Barbara has called
the California ballot length preposterous and labeled
the overuse of the initiative process deplorable. UCLA
political scientist Winston Crouch once blamed the
California constitution for the trouble; that 1879
document started life as the third longest thing of its
kind in the world, and it has since been ballooned by
more than three hundred amendments.

I think we force ourselves to do more choosing in
the West because we don't trust our elected leaders to
choose for us. We prefer professional actors to political
axemen. We tolerate mavericks but not machines. We

175

have a history of radicalism and conservatism and splinterism that makes us unlike our more stable Eastern brethern. We also have fewer crooks in high places. And maybe that's why we don't want to be as neatly packaged, politically, as New York and Massachusetts and Pennsylvania.

During Joseph Alioto's unsuccessful run for the governorship in 1974, his wife ran away in the middle of the primary campaign. The first lady of San Francisco went into hiding; it was the first time a married major candidate had to admit that he couldn't find his livingmate. Law-enforcement agencies were called into the act. Media correspondents hovered around like buzzards. Oppnents didn't know whether to make an issue out of Mrs. Alioto or count their own blessings in their own bedrooms.

Angelina Alioto reappeared of her own accord. There hadn't been any foul play, she said; there hadn't been any hanky or panky. She was simply sick of the part, sick of being a prop at political banquets, sick of having to run behind the bandwagons, sick of being used without being consulted. She came back, she said, because she still believed in her husband, but she needed some time off to be herself.

California responded in a variety of ways—which is the usual California response. The Women's Movement claimed Angelina Alioto as a rightful sister. The liberal community went cluck-cluck in public and enjoyed a few chuckles in private. The moderates were generally sympathetic rather than cruel. The conservatives could empathize with the mayor. In short, Joseph Alioto neither gained nor suffered politically from his wife's unprecedented leave of absence. He finished the race about where he started, behind Gerry Brown's household name.

That little bit of high drama summarizes the California tolerance for individuals who insist that the player is more important than the team. That tolerance extends to everything we do out here. Such acceptance is not offered in the East, especially when the East is asked to accept us as we are. Easterners don't understand runaways who carry their optimism with them.

-XII-

Don't Tilt Us Anymore

The great American misunderstanding between East and West is largely a function of the media. The media muck things up. The media mostly live in the East and fail to communicate an honest view of the West. Maybe "honest" is the wrong word. They fail to communicate an accurate or fair or intelligent view of the West.

Let us begin with a specific example of Eastern nearsightedness as demonstrated in the summer of '74 by *Time* magazine. *Time* is neither the worst offender in media myopia nor the best force of journalistic reform. But *Time* is still the most influential newsmagazine in the United States, and even Californians read it with grudging respect. In July of 1974, the editors of *Time* published a special supplement on leadership in America—not a bad idea, considering the way we were all wallowing in Watergate blues, plunging stock market, and galloping inflation. Part of the supplement was a national portfolio of potential leaders, women and men forty-five years old and younger.

". . . Time correspondents last April began gathering recommendations from university presidents and professors, Congressmen, church figures, industrialists," the magazine explained. "The editors trimmed, amended, sifted and resifted the lengthy list that resulted. What follows is not—and was not intended to be—a reflection of the geographic, political, racial or sexual makeup of America."

The disclaimer doesn't ease *Time* off the hook. A national survey is a national survey, and if it wasn't an attempt to name important names from all over, then the whole business was balderdash.

The results, disclaimer or not, were astonishing.

Of the two hundred Americans honored with leadership responsibility, ninety-nine live in the Northeast corner of the country. While it is possible that half our important people make their homes in about 10 percent of our available space, the resultant portrait of America leaves a short-legged South, a concave Midwest, and an appendage West.

More remarkable was the number of New Yorkers included: thirty-one. Are we, we who don't choose to sleep and work in the biggest, beastliest city in the United States, ready to believe that more than 15 percent of our upcoming leaders occupy such a small piece of American property?

Three locations dominated the survey: New York

(thirty-one), Washington, D.C. (twenty), and Massachusetts (sixteen) accounted for more than two thirds of the East's ninety-nine leaders.

California, in contrast, has the same number of *Time*-picked leaders as has Massachusetts. Massachusetts, with fewer than six million bodies, shelters as many supposed celebrities as California, with more than twenty million bodies. I won't argue that Massachusetts, with all its history, doesn't have a tradition for spawning greatness. But I work my way through the leadership laundry list with a rising feeling that nearness to New York is more important than background in the Back Bay. Massachusetts has Boston and all those schools and all those hospitals. The *Time* list pays respects to Harvard, Wellesley, MIT, and Radcliffe. If Washington logically weighs in with politicians and New York with business names, Massachusetts shines with educators and theorists.

The funny part of the California people is the preponderance of politicians. Half of the sixteen selections are full-time political animals, and three others are famous for their dealings with government; six of the sixteen are elected officials.

Not one business person, in the usual sense, was named from California.

Only two people connected with education made the ranks. William Banowsky, president of Pepperdine University, was one. Pepperdine does not have a national reputation, but it does have a healthy endowment from conservative philanthropists, and President Banowsky has become something of a celebrity for his off-campus appearances as a Republican spokesman and media personality. Murray Gell-Mann, the Nobel

180

physicist from Cal-Tech, was the other. Gell-Mann alone represents California higher education; there were no choices from Berkeley, Stanford, UCLA, the Claremont Colleges, or the dozens of other institutions that have distinguished faculties and facilities.

The opportunity for public higher education is broader and deeper in California than anywhere else in the United States. The California complex of state university campuses, state colleges and community colleges is a model for the world. But *Time* could find a public educator to honor.

Only one person from the social sciences came from California. Michael Murphy, a co-founder of the Esalen Institute, was *Time's* choice—a reasonable choice, although an obvious one. Esalen not only deserves its reputation as a birthplace of the human-potential movement, it has also been the tourist attraction for hundreds of East Coast writers who wanted to find convenient explanations for openness, communal bathing, body awareness, affective education, and encounter grouping. Esalen was a picturesque place to go, hanging off the cliffs at Big Sur, offering several experts on openness who were willing to be interviewed at the drop of a masthead. I don't quarrel with the importance of what Murphy wrought, but I quibble with the herding instincts of New York journalists who follow in one another's footsteps, believing only what they read in one another's dispatches, rediscovering one another's researches.

Only one California media creature was included. Jann Wenner, *Rolling Stone's* precocious under-thirty publisher, indeed built a book and a magazine empire on the shaky foundations of rock music. But where

181

were the Californians who publish for audiences twice the size of Wenner's, the Californians who dominate television, the Californians who supposedly define lifestyle for the rest of the country? It so happens that *Time* has an excellent bureau in California, high above the material splendor of Beverly Hills. Its correspondents have a working knowledge of the state and the media in it. But I'll bet the home office finds their recommendations suspect precisely because those correspondents are living in the West on a day-to-day basis—they've been tainted by the terrain.

No one from the entertainment industry was named at all. Another *Time* disclaimer doesn't quite tell us why: "What indeed was our criterion? The touchstone was civic or social impact. That automatically included politicians and government officials, as well as businessmen, educators, lawyers, scientists, journalists. The definition ruled out many Americans who are truly outstanding in their fields but who really belong in another category. They exemplify what John Gardner describes as 'virtuoso leadership'—the diva, the poet or novelist, painter or actor. They may be a fresh inspiration and their audiences may be vast, but they are basically soloists, and we felt they should be included only if their work had a clear, direct impact on society."

I suppose locking out the poets and novelists is arguable as well as arbitrary. But what has more direct impact on society than any other facet of American enterprise? The amusement field, including television and records and movies and mass concerts. And where does this field call home? California. If *Time* could include sports figures, which it did, then *Time* should have curtsied a couple of times toward the producers and directors of popular arts. The movies are certainly not solo efforts, but involve massive combinations of talents to reach mass audiences around the world. The makers of motion pictures and television programs are the most influential translators of life in the universe. Even their myths have social impact. Poor *Time* seemed to think television's clout begins and ends with the national news plus a few words from the New York–based folks who work for public broadcasting. That's what happens when you live in a cruel climate where you have to look serious in order to be taken seriously.

My colleague from California, Digby Diehl, saw a similar sort of media incest at the National Book Awards for 1974, which are invariably held in New York. Most of the winners were from New York. "But it was not until Murray Kempton approached me later," wrote Diehl from the scene of the celebrations, "that I realized just how parochial the situation is. 'This year is a victory for the West Side,' he exclaimed. For a moment I was confused, thinking that in the context of these national awards, Kempton was referring to those who live on the wrong side of the Mississippi. What he actually meant was that the preponderance of winners came from the west side of the island of Manhattan, thus being a slap in the face to the high-class east side of the island which is the traditional neighborhood for well-to-do writers. I was stunned; he was seriously talking about America's only national literary awards as some kind of intramural game played within the confines of that 22 square miles of rock. I was further enlightened that four of the winners all lived in the same building at 333 Central Park West, along with many of the publishing industry's most important figures."

Diehl, the book editor for the Los Angeles *Times,* went on to report one cause of such literary insularity on Manhattan Island, quoting a *New York Times* story that traced the marriages, love liaisons, and living arrangements shared by the people in the trade. New York literary creatures are literally bound together. He wrote, ". . . in New York, this wry confession seems very funny. But to the thousands of writers and editors staring at the doors of that closed shop, an analysis of that Manhattan in-club is outrageous.

"Another part of the answer," Diehl continued, "must be sought in the embarrassing acceptance speech that Karen Brazell made from the podium at Lincoln Center's Alice Tully Hall upon receiving a National Book Award in translation. Her final words expressed gratitude to her former Columbia University teacher and friend Donald Keene. Professor Keene is a member of the jury which gave Brazell the award."

Diehl wound up his outrage from the outside by calling for the nationalization of the National Book Awards, demanding juries with membership west of the Hudson River. He reminded me of something the late Nat Cole said when complaining about the deafness of Tin Pan Alley: "None of those people ever heard anything on the other side of the Holland Tunnel."

The malady Diehl describes in the book business is the one afflicting all the media. And it has two symptoms that mutually aggravate each other. One involves the incest rampant in New York, publishing headquarters for the country. In-breeding is bad for the species, tending to produce more temperamental strains who bleed too easily and see too restrictedly. The other is the infectious nature of the sick incestors. They have extraordinary powers of circulation, distribution, and communication. What New Yorkers say of California receives more attention than what Californians say of their own turf. The Eastern media, like overstaying mothers-in-law, tend to dwell on what they want to criticize in the West, arriving with preconceptions, staying with archaic perceptions, and going home to broadcast misinterpretations. Language does alter reality, and sometimes sensitive Californians believe they are as New Yorkers see them rather than as they are.

In 1967, I tried to separate the Eastern treatment of California into three stages:

The first, or nut-puncture period, owed its popularity to the movies and reached its greatest popularity in the forties and fifties. Remember? California was where all the loose nuts slid to from more rooted sections of the United States . . . Los Angeles was where the lotus eaters lived, and when they forsook flowers it was for mushroomburgers or organic frankfurters at the nearby goat's milk drive-in. Los Angeles was really Hollywood anyway. And Hollywood was nowhere, a region of myth that drove actors into cults or pushed sensitive writers, like Scott Fitzgerald, into their graves. What could a self-respecting magazine say about Southern California that wasn't derogatory? Almost nothing. If we weren't funny, we were outrageous. New York editors refused to believe there was more to this place than the sticky trickle of orange juice and the bulge of wet-mouthed maidens. When a correspondent reported otherwise, the home office promptly decided that the man or woman had been infected by the same virus that demented other sun worshippers. Nut puncturing, while no longer the dominant practice, has never quite died, either. As recently as 1965, John Ciardi wrote for the *Saturday Review* a column called "Foamrubbersville" and worried: "I'm not sure, in fact, but what one should go through all of Los Angeles with one psychic eye closed. The only possible mistake is in trying to perceive depth there." . . . In 1962, *Newsweek* was still saying, "Los Angeles has women in tight fuchsia slacks, Bible Belt evangelism and searchlights spearing the sky for every custard-stand opening."

I had lived in California for only eight years when I wrote the piece for *West* magazine. But I had already been a correspondent for two Eastern-based national publications, and the reference to what home offices thought was a whimper from my own experience. At both *Life* and *Saturday Evening Post,* there had been mammoth appetites for stories from California. The trouble was the narrowness of those appetites and the simplicity of those tastes. Show-biz stories were welcome, especially if they contained a few bustlines. Aviation or aerospace suggestions were well received; a sense of duty and patriotism acknowledged that California's wild blue yonder was important to everyone's sense of security or gee whiz. And the bizarre almost never failed, because Eastern editors never tired of California as the national capital of human crazy quilts.

Political stories, however, were difficult to offer home offices. So were education stories. And architectural stories and business stories and land-use stories and even pure science stories. If it didn't wear a bathing suit, then it could hardly come from California. I remember one turndown in particular, when a Los Angeles writer asked me to query the Eastern headquarters on a possible article about Ronald Reagan, the one-time actor who was just beginning to make a name for himself in politics as an after-chicken speaker on the Republican banquet circuit. No, said New York. No one will ever hear of Reagan again unless they rerun *Bedtime for Bonzo* on late-night television.

After the nut-puncture period came the deification of demography, when California was recognized as the most populous state in the Union. It was regrettable but it was fact, and the national magazines took turns putting special issues together on the subject of how big the West had become. *Life's* issue of October 1962 was typical: "California is not all great, as any new arrival will tell you. But this is a time for paean, for accolade, a time to admire and be amazed." *Boom* was still a happy sound anywhere in America. Writer Ernest Havemann stationed himself at the border and interviewed immigrants as they drove away from the old heritage into the California incubator: "They have arrived impelled by necessity or lured by a dream. They have pursued the rainbow, as far as they can, to the rim of the U.S. They like what they see at first glance or hate it. Most of them—statistics show—will stay."

And *Look* was the magazine that quickly saw California as "a window into the future" in 1962. "California technology," I wrote in *West,* "for good or evil, emerged as the tool to fix a leaky future . . . Incredible. The refugees were suddenly supposed to save the old homestead." The idea of giving California responsibility for saving the United States was novel to New York. It was also tempting. The editors could sit back there like old Britons and write funny commentaries on how the brash upstarts were behaving.

Clifton Fadiman did one of the more graceful pieces of the period, for *Holiday.* Fadiman lived in California by then, and had better credentials than a week in the Fairmont Hotel followed by a week in the Bel-Air. "Writing about most American cities," began Fadiman in a section on Los Angeles, "is like writing a biography of Chester A. Arthur. It can be done but why do it? New York, Boston, San Francisco are moderately write-aboutable. Denver, Detroit are the Chester A. Arthur of cities. But Los Angeles stands alone, interminably discussable. Some writers are drawn to it as one's fingernails to an itch; others, because like the illusionist's performance, it teases the mind; others because all startling growths, whether of an organism or an anthill, fascinate." Then Fadiman wrote, "Unyokable adjectives fit L.A.—drab, surprising; absurd, impressive; politically conservative, politically experimental. A paradise of paradox."

"Paradise of paradox" looks like more alliteration than the law should allow these days, but in 1962 the phrase became a major sub-theme of California's treatment from the outside. If it couldn't be labeled easily, then it had to be a place of contradictions. It was. But even contradictions confused some of the authors in stage two. William Graves of the *National Geographic* (based in Washington, D.C., not New York) managed to find an intrastate rivalry between San Francisco and Los Angeles, but he turned the story upside down: "Los Angeles, like many giants, often suffers the taunts of a world built to slightly smaller scale. Even Californians make fun of their colossus. 'Los Angeles,' runs the quip, 'speaks unkindly of San Francisco but San Francisco never mentions Los Angeles at all.' "

Absolutely wrong. San Franciscans are the ones who constantly disparage Los Angeles, often using old Philadelphia jokes, such as the one about the first prize in a contest being two free days in L.A. and the second prize a whole week in L.A. Los Angeles people claim to like San Francisco.

Phase three of the Eastern view of the West started in the later sixties, with the human-potential movement. George Leonard did it in *Look*. And Leonard, an early habitué of Esalen, knew the subject. If he was too close to being rhapsodic about what he called the "turned-on people," it was because probably he was too close to being one of them. But being too close is better than being foreign; California had always suffered from hit-and-run journalism in the past.

Richard Todd, for *Harper's*, followed Leonard within half a year under the heading "Turned-on and Super-Sincere in California." Todd looked at the open-pore, open-soul approach to human relations and came away uncomfortable: "Outside in the air," he wrote after one encounter session, "you discover that you have a distinctly uncomfortable feeling, as if you had been kissed against your will."

That's pretty much my feeling about the California treatment as administered by New York editor-analysts. At the end of the 1967 article I tried to sum up a slight case of indigestion after tasting dozens of magazine stories on the West: "If the examiners have missed any single important quirk in our entire system, it is that we are volunteeers, more than 90 per cent of us. Whatever ails us, we have brought upon ourselves. Unlike most bodies in most other places, Californians consciously made their beds and remain content to thrash in them. The most pervasive symptom of our whole society is that we grant everyone else the privacy and mobility to find his own well-being—or his own growing pains. Other places change with time. California changes with transfusions of new blood. Let them sit back there and chart our fevers. A volunteer doesn't really expect to be understood."

I wouldn't take back those words today. But I'm less gracious about the New York diagnoses than I used to be. What seems to have happened in the last six or seven years is a media attempt to make California conform to the aspirations assigned it by the media. A major motive for my writing this complaint is to yell for less help. Please don't tilt us any more. Don't give us responsibility for making America something else, for saving something that used to live somewhere else or for organizing twenty-first-century survival tactics. We're refugees, remember. We came out here to make a clean getaway. Our optimism is partly relief, relief that we're not your children anymore. Stop sending orders from the old country.

I think we were better off in the old days, as punctured provincials. The East didn't expect much from us then, other than amusement. We were their butts, the ridiculous rump convention of a continent some three thousand miles away, the jesters who were tolerated because they sent funny pictures and performed silly social gestures. It's easier to be a joke than to be responsible.

California's attempts to become a media empire in its own right have generally failed, mainly because California hasn't really tried to address the national audience.

Oh, there have been a few flurries of publishing pretensions. The beat school that grew up around San Francisco's North Beach gave the outside world some poetry and some Kerouac. But poetry is about as popular as eggplant with mass appetites. Sherbourne Press in Los Angeles made a stab at competing with the big book boys during the sixties, issuing a grab bag of good stuff and dirty stuff and good and dirty stuff. But the big Eastern houses could churn out similar materials with much better distribution arrangements. Southern California's best house was Ward Ritchie Press. But it concentrated on Californian and cook books. And it made most of its profits by job printing. Ward Ritchie was sold to a distribution outfit in the early seventies. Now firms with such interesting names as Wollstonecraft, Tarcher, and Camaro are trying to bind California into a book business all its own.

Sunset Publishing is the big success story; *Sunset* magazine and Sunset books make millions and appeal to millions. They are exquisitely helpful in such matters as azalea cultivation, backyard barbecuing, off-trail touring, and slump-fence building. Sunset offers Western service to a population immersed in all manner of personal how-to. Along the way, Sunset is also a major force for conservation and open-space protection, but the publications are guidebooks rather than crusades.

The angriest little respectable magazine in the state is called *Cry California,* published by California Tomorrow, a non-profit San Francisco corporation. *Cry California* originally coined the term "slurb" to cover the ugly ground where the residential projects sprawl to infinity, where lack of land planning has produced tracts with no esthetic attraction or redeeming social virtues. California Tomorrow also produced a remarkable state plan in the seventies, full of land-use reform and political reform and social consciousness. It was embraced by academicians and even a few bureaucrats as an extraordinary exercise in big thinking. Politicians, however, pretended it didn't exist. They knew that Californians were unaccustomed to public planning.

California's major electronic media are enslaved to the New York networks and the Eastern order of priorities. Earlier I mentioned Tom Brokaw, a one-time Los Angeles anchorman who was transferred to Washington, D.C., as NBC's White House correspondent. The network considered the switch a major promotion, figuring that any important newsperson would rather speak from the capital's streets than the center of a studio in the provinces.

Media people continue to go to New York to make their fortune, if fortune-making is what they want. The young writers or broadcasters who choose to settle in California—and stay there—tend to be more interested in making a life than a living.

The dominant newspaper in California is the Los Angeles *Times.* It earns more advertising revenue than any other paper in the country. Its circulation is second only to that of the tabloid *Daily News* of New York. Its standing in the trade, for editorial quality, is alongside that of *The New York Times* and the *Washington Post* as one of the three best dailies in the nation. I like it. But I also work for it, and any further admiration offered here may be considered suspect.

There was a moment of major change for the Los Angeles *Times,* however, that is pertinent here. In the early sixties, right about the time that California was boasting more bodies than New York, *The New York Times* launched the daily West Coast edition described earlier. The prospect of such competition caused the L.A. *Times* to begin its own expansion, by hiring people, by opening new bureaus, by broadening its own editorial policy to approach a position of staunch moderation. Good things happened to the paper in the process, internal things independent of *The New York Times*'s incursion. The news service spawned by cooperative efforts of the L.A. *Times* and the *Washington Post* became a distinguished source of reportage. The L.A. *Times* developed investigative staffs, interpretive staffs, special-interest staffs. The L.A. *Times* grew from a good, rich newspaper into an extremely good, extremely rich newspaper.

Meanwhile, the West Coast edition of *The New York Times* floundered. It was born and died before many people had noticed; it died of East Coast mentality. The home office spent barrels of dollars on production facilities and ad-sale promotion, but hardly any money on enlarged editorial vision. The *NYT* stuck a branch in the Western ground without providing any real roots for coverage. When the Western edition flopped, the L.A. *Times* had already become good enough to compete, in quality terms, with the old Eastern edition.

Two magazines have made a national dent from the West. *Rolling Stone,* out of San Francisco, is the rock journal run by young Jann Wenner of *Time* magazine's "Two Hundred" fame. *Psychology Today,* out of little Del Mar, is the behavioral success story that capitalized on excellent art direction and an ability to translate the growth of shrinkage in America.

I suppose both interests, the rock culture and the behavioral obsession, are appropriate to California. San Francisco was where the flower children bloomed and then became other kinds of hybrids. La Jolla, near Del Mar, was where Carl Rogers and other explorers of encounter groups began such wondrously named institutions as the Center for the Study of the Person and the Western Behavioral Sciences Institute. Marathon concerts and marathon sensitivity groups were equally at home in the Bay Area and Southern California.

Rolling Stone has grown in recent years, from a one-track—or eight-track—music mind to include politics, sociology, and investigative reporting in its ad-rich pages. The writing tends to be rich and aural, with debts to the Tom Wolfe school of ugga-ugga-whump-whump typography. But it is literary in its own way, and if the youth culture used *Rolling Stone* as its style guide to maturity, national grace and spelling would be exponentially improved.

Psychology Today has changed owners almost as regularly as snakes change skins, but the editorial direction remains faithful toward matters of the mind, uncouched so laymen will understand. Slick, hip, reasonably candid, *Psychology Today* is as immersed in therapy trends as *Rolling Stone* is based on chord changes in pluck and luck.

Psychology Today has been so successful, in fact, that it inspired a Southern California competitor called *Human Behavior*, which takes a departmentalized page from *Time*'s format and applies it to psychological subjects. *Human Behavior* is deft, brisk, and less splashy than *Psychology Today*, drawing the bulk of its material from the thousands of current academic studies in the social sciences and then enlivening the findings in more human language.

Some of the West's best periodicals are parochial, either named after cities or named after the special geographic interests they embrace. They are generally satisfying as what they are, California journals aimed at particular California targets. But *Los Angeles* magazine, for instance, will never be *New York* magazine. *Los Angeles* readers have an honest interest in what absorbs people who live in the center of gravity. *New York* readers wouldn't deign to give a damn about day-to-day life in what's supposed to be the city of the future.

Eastern media snobbery has been rampant ever since I've been in the business on both coasts. Possibly my memory of the Democratic National Convention of 1960 tells the whole story of opposite attitudes. I worked for *Life* then, in Los Angeles, as a correspondent. The *Life* bureau was big—eight reporters and four photographers. The story was also big—the emergence of John F. Kennedy as a candidate for President.

I was young, impressionable, eager, and prepared to work twenty-hour days. So I was pleased when the

195

bureau chief, on instructions from the home office, ordered all of us correspondents and photographers to live in a downtown hotel for the duration of the convention. We would be available around the clock that way. We would be within reasonable driving distance of the dramatics at the convention arena and the deals at the major delegations' hotels. No matter that my home was only fifteen minutes farther away; the idea of being interned was appealing, a proof of how important was our temporary place in history. Some of the older bureau hands complained about the inconvenience of uprooting. I was sure they had been around too long and were merely malingering.

Then the Washington bureau came to town. They too would cover the convention.

Then the New York editors came to town. They too would cover the convention.

After all, the Washington people were the ones who knew all the stars: Kennedy and Johnson and Stevenson and Eleanor Roosevelt.

After all, the New York people were the ones who made magazine policy and decided what weight to give which story. The Washington people and the New York people and the Los Angeles people met one night for a massive party in the Biltmore Hotel, one big happy drunken raucous journalistic family. I was still delighted.

Delight began to fade on the first day of the proceedings. My assignment was to cover a caucus of the Idaho delegation. The Idaho delegation had only a handful of votes and a thimbleful of arguments. Idaho wasn't being courted seriously by any of the major candidates, because they knew where Idaho was already. The caucus was both inane and unnewsworthy; party functionaries delivered functional speeches on housekeeping matters amidst the L.A. sprawl.

While I was attending Idaho, the people from Washington and the people from New York were covering the states that mattered: Texas, New York, Illinois, Pennsylvania, Michigan, and California. They were covering California because, after all, this was a national story, and California couldn't be left to the *Life* people who lived there.

The second day, I was assigned the Minnesota caucus. It wasn't dull at all, because Minnesota turned out to have three potential vice-presidential candidates: Hubert Humphrey, as ever; Eugene McCarthy, as liberal upstart; Orville Freeman, as farm expert. I had a fine time watching the three powers from one state politic among their own partisans, dealing and dividing. And I sat down at the typewriter that night to describe it all.

The editors were interested. So they assigned Minnesota to an Eastern expert the next day. And I was sent to Iowa, a Siberia only one degree warmer than Idaho.

My California colleagues were faring no better. The Los Angeles bureau was moving into such caucuses as Wyoming, New Hampshire, Nevada, Nebraska, and New Mexico—wherever the vote was light and the arguments unimportant.

And we became slightly more resentful when we discovered that some of the New York and Washington people had brought their wives with them. To keep them company at night. To use up valuable floor passes originally intended for working press. To attend cocktail parties. Here we were, separated from home and family because of the urgency of the situation, even though home and family were just a couple of miles up the road. And here they were, with wives in tow, staying in more comfortable hotel rooms. Here we were, standing up to our ears in Idaho potatoes and Iowa corn. Here they were, rubbing elbows with potential Presidents. Here we were, the hosts being ordered around by the guests in our own town.

One of the more exciting moments of that most exciting convention was the demonstration, so beautifully organized it looked spontaneous, for Adlai Stevenson. The Stevenson diehards had managed to smuggle hundreds of non-delegates into the Sports Arena so that at the magic moment—of nomination, of Eleanor Roosevelt's blessing from the gallery, of television's concentration—these impassioned masses could make a proper spectacle of themselves. The Hollywood folks had lent their names and bodies to the effort. The Stevenson spectacle was a grass-roots production number orchestrated by directors and producers who knew exactly how to do it. *Life*'s movie experts in Los Angeles knew what was going on, but movie experts are not consulted on matters of national policy. If the Washington and New York people hadn't been so insistent about stealing every scene, the L.A. bureau could have made the convention make more sense to the audience.

That was the week I realized I couldn't have what seemed to be the best of both American worlds: an East Coast employer and a West Coast home address. If I wanted to stay with Time Incorporated, then I'd have to work my way back to New York and Washington. If

I wanted to remain in California, I'd have to quit the company, because nobody worth his paycheck is allowed to live forever in the provinces. There's supposed to be something wrong with an employee who doesn't choose to live at the home office, in the corporate lap.

One of the explanations for why the media muck things up is that attitude. The media leaders of the East really believe that stories begin and end where *they* are, not necessarily where the stories are. Serious media are supposed to live on the east side of the Hudson River. The West Coast is allowed to have the amusement media.

California gradually became the foam bed of situation comedy, the base for Johnny Carson's after-hours conversations and the prime location for horse operas, cop operas, and daytime game operas. The move was somewhat grudging, but Hollywood was still where the movie people were, and the movie people were only too happy to work for television during the long droughts between pictures.

Such a division of television responsibilities suits the East Coast fine nowadays. Cronkite is in New York. Carson is in Los Angeles. The news is distributed from Manhattan. The crap is filmed in Hollywood. The Atlantic is where the weight is. The Pacific is full of froth.

And the view of California media from a New York high-rise is usually distorted with respect to San Francisco in relation to Los Angeles. The sophistication of San Francisco is an article of faith in Manhattan. The restaurants, you know, the beloved begloved women, you know, the cosmopolitan pedestrian crowd, you know. The truth is that San Francisco may have all those reported virtues, but not much else is reported there. The San Francisco newspapers are big on gossip and small on news, dealing with the city and the world as one fat feature story. San Francisco's television news coverage, excepting the local public-broadcasting channel, is also illuminated by more sweetness than light. The smaller city in California is the pettier city in California, tourist applause notwithstanding. Los Angeles, even with its overdose of show biz, offers the local audience more information and more substance than what the media dredge up around the Bay.

I have come to be at peace with being a provincial, because there are freedoms allowed in direct proportion to the distance from the seat of power.

But there are still days when I wish I could deliver mandates to my old media friends in New York, mandates that might help them write truer or say better things about their bumpkin colleagues on the Coast. I even have a handy list:

1. Do not consider sunshine to be a sin unto itself. Lives of stimuli and seriousness can be pursued in a comfortable climate. One doesn't have to hear the readings of the latest wind-chill factor in order to know that the world is not easy.

2. Do not forget that the California refugees once made a conscious decision to make their moves. If the center of the universe had been habitable for all, then you might have never had to deal with California.

3. Do not expect us to find West Coast solutions for East Coast problems. Do not expect us to be the "test bed for tomorrow" simply because you stamped us that way on your sheets.

200

4. Do not make a big thing of asking what we do at night. We usually do whatever we feel like doing, and do not enjoy elaborate plans made in advance. We are not as easily bored as you are, hence we require less structure.

5. Do not visit us with your preconceptions or your editor's preconceptions. Come as you are, and try to see us as we are.

6. Do not be too clever about our bad air, our bad traffic, or our bad dope problem. Yours are worse.

7. But also, do not lose your supercilious attitude entirely. We need to have East Coast chauvinists for our own protection.

8. And, above all, do not blame us for the crisis in American confidence. We may be sillier than you are, but it wasn't silliness that gave us Watergate, inflation, or armed cabdrivers. I think those contributions to the culture came from your shore. We will not save your world for you, but we manage to stay hopeful, because we rely on individuals more than we rely on institutions. You folks worry about the team. We'll try to take care of ourselves.

-XIII-

The Motion Movement

I made myself a note about East-West differences in
time and space and distance, automobiles aside: "The
East has a need to know where it is and who its people
are. The West thrives on the obliteration of traditional
dimensions. Easterners are identified by place, geogra-
phically and sociologically. Westerners, with the possible exception of San Franciscans, refuse loyalty to
anywhere."

Then, during the course of this book, I flew from
Oakland to Los Angeles one Sunday, and on arrival
was astonished to see an airline stewardess leading
seven small children from the plane. There were four
white kids, two black ones, and one brown—all apparently unrelated. I watched the stewardess deliver each
of the children to a different adult waiting in the airport. These young travelers, all under twelve years of

age, and some looking to be less than eight, had come to Southern California by themselves that day, with an airline acting as chaperone.

It seemed significant that nearly 10 percent of a flight's passenger list included unescorted minors. I can't imagine so much youthful mobility between Boston and Washington.

The airline itself is somewhat significant. Pacific Southwest Airlines operates wholly within California borders, managing to make a living by serving eleven cities within a single state—including San Francisco, L.A., San Diego, Sacramento, Oakland, and San Jose. The airline commuter is enough of a California commonplace to sustain such a business, even in competition with interstate truck carriers such as United and Western, which work similar routes.

PSA worked to California's advantage in the sixties, driving intrastate prices down because PSA didn't have to live within the regulations established by the federal government for flying between states. United and Western were forced to join PSA in offering bargain fares between San Francisco and Los Angeles, at one time as little as twenty-five dollars for a round trip distance of nearly one thousand miles. Tickets have risen in price with inflation, but the run between Northern and Southern California remains one of the least expensive ways to travel at five hundred miles an hour in the entire world.

PSA is also peculiarly Californian in its promotional style, with a bald appeal to the rootless businessman in every advertising detail down to the stewardesses' uniforms. The friendly young woman who took those children in tow was wearing the standard

PSA flight suit: a pair of tight red leather boots ending just below the knee, a red-pink-orange microskirt ending just below the crotch, a pair of red hot pants underneath the skirt, and a torso-fitting tunic of the same three inflammable colors.

Critics have said the PSA cabin staff look like hookers. The airline itself exploits its women as if they were starlets, sending them off to ribbon cuttings, sports events, and commercial fairs to make decorative appearances. While the national Women's Movement has excoriated National Airlines for its "Fly Me" campaign and blasted Continental Airlines for the advertisements boasting "we really move our tails for you," PSA has blithely gone about its California business using employees as aisle objects. Eastern and American Airlines would never dare dress crews that way, not with so many Congressmen for commuters.

PSA has its own monthly publication, called *California* magazine, "edited exclusively for the more than 7 million passengers who annually fly Pacific Southwest Airlines." Characteristically, a pretty girl consistently graces the cover, often in a neckline style made famous by *Cosmopolitan*. A feature called "Californians" has a subhead, "Interesting citizens of the nation state." And there is some of that geographic chauvinism operating among people of the West, a feeling of being part of bigness. But if Californians puff up about living as separate citizens of a nation-state, they don't bring the loyalty down to levels of city, neighborhood, or street. That would seem parochial.

PSA has painted its planes in red, orange, and pink, dubbed them the unofficial state birds of California, and drawn large smiles just below the aircraft noses. Now, all of the above does tend to create a festive sort of atmosphere for flying—the grinning jets, the carnival color scheme, and the booted maidens with their cantilevered eyelashes. None of it suggests the exquisite precision of technology or flight safety; PSA probably figures its passengers take mach speeds and high altitude for granted.

A 1974 issue of *California* magazine emphasized, appropriately enough, the conflict between coasts. Writer Richard Pietschmann claimed to be fed up with Eastern chauvinism: "It is time once again to rub New York's nose in . . . well, in New York." He interviewed five sets of refugees from the East, to discover that almost all of them had common migratory patterns: "(1) their original move to California was followed by a short return to New York before moving back here for good; (2) they wanted to escape the cold; (3) all retain a good deal of the New Yorker in them; (4) women miss their friends and family; (5) an astonishing number of their old New York friends now also live in California." An adman told Pietschmann, "I decided I wasn't going to die in New York . . . I knew I had to come here." A San Francisco planner said California is a pleasanter place to live. A cabbie claimed he couldn't relax in New York. And movie actor James Caan bragged about the amount of outdoor activity in the West.

None of the PSA transplants mentioned distance, but the nation-state notion can be applied to one hunk of geography that stretches from ocean to desert, from Mexico to Oregon, about nine hundred miles up the landfall without a border in between.

California tourist attractions echo the theme in a burst of exuberance and imitation. The whole world has almost been recreated in California, because

California has the room and greed to make it possible. The Matterhorn is at Disneyland in Anaheim, and the mock Matterhorn—made sturdily enough for real mountain climbing—is better known than the original. There's a Japanese Deer Park not far away in Orange County. London Bridge was rebuilt, stone by stone, at Lake Havasu, a real-estate promotion along the Arizona-California border. The *Queen Mary,* intact, was bought by the city of Long Beach to be permanently berthed as a tourist hotel with smokestacks. Lion Country Safari carried wild beasts to a grazing land near Laguna.

There's an arrogance in all this, of course: the arrogance of affluence and Hollywood-style promotion. Why go to the real thing when you can recreate the real thing within a statewide studio and charge for admission?

There's a sort of chauvinism growing up around the California wine industry, reflected in prices for homegrown varietals such as Cabernet Sauvignon, now corked at prices of nine and ten dollars a bottle. Westerners touring Europe have been seen complaining about the lack of Napa Valley wine in Paris—a sure indication that we have spawned a creature called the Ugly Californian.

I happen to admire California wines, and admit to drinking them in more than moderation on festive occasions. I also allow that I find California grape superior to those grown in New York or Ohio for pressing purposes. But just because California was able to stick Cabernets and Chardonnays and Pinot Noirs in the ground, transplanting them much like the *Queen Mary,* doesn't justify our insistence on finding them better than the homegrown variety in France.

The arrogance of the grape has a new kinship with show business at Sterling Vineyards, a winery newly built on a knoll above the Napa Valley. A traditional California treat, for northerners and southerners alike, was a day's drive through the wine country, where the growers conducted guided tours of their fields and vats and then offered visitors a free tasting session. The wines were also offered for sale after the tasting, but no tourist was under any buying pressure. Such wineries as BV, Charles Krug, and Robert Mondavi—the big names—continue such gracious public-relations gestures, and thousands of Californians continue to find themselves in a fermented condition between the towns of Oakville and St. Helena. Sterling, near the top of the grape run, also invites visitors; it's included in the brochure listing wineries that welcome tourists. And Sterling, from the state highway, appears to be one of the more exciting stops. The winery is angular and alabaster, looking like a modern monastery overseeing the valley floor. One drives down a tree-lined entry road until one comes to a cable car. The cable car is the commercial hitch: The tourist must pay two dollars for a ride up the knoll—and not a long ride at that—just to have the privilege of taking an industry tour. Sterling wines happen to be excellent, but there's a distinct aftertaste about the operation, suggesting that the proprietors may be more interested in squeezing travelers than grapes.

It is possible and pleasurable to spend two or three weeks within California's borders, covering two hundred fifty or three hundred miles a day and moving from ocean to mountain to arid plain to mineral springs to tropical garden to wind-bitten cliff. If the entrepreneurs have reconstructed the Old World within one state, nature had already dumped most of her weather and topography and best scenery inside the same big piece of geography.

On the East Coast, moving two hundred fifty miles a day takes a traveler through several states in a few days, whether going up, down, or across. New England and the Mid-Atlantic states are somewhat like Europe in the relationship between abutting borders. One knows when he has left Connecticut for New York, New York for New Jersey, and New Jersey for Pennsylvania—not simply by roadsigns, but by distinct differences in the personality of the commerce or the people. The East is crowded, and it seems important in the East to establish identity from geography. Let us take, for homely example, the unbrotherly boroughs of Brooklyn and the Bronx. The people speak the same language in both places—or almost the same classic Sheldon Leonard dialect. Their origins are similar, including large inputs of Irish, Italian, Jewish, and black citizen blocs. Brooklyn and the Bronx both belong to New York City, and the residents could properly call themselves New Yorkers if they wanted to. But they prefer to identify with their particular borough. And then they slice the borough down to specific neighborhoods within that small dense universe. People say they come from the East Bronx, as opposed to the West Bronx. Almost like illegal street-gang members, perfectly respectable citizens of Brooklyn or the Bronx identify with small pieces of turf on which they feel at home and with friends—as opposed to New York at large, in which they feel threatened and alien. And no Brooklyn body would ever want to be confused with a Bronx one.

The same sort of territorial imperative operates in fancier areas of the East. Bryn Mawr draws lines against Villanova, although both share the Main Line. Scarsdale would never want to be confused with White Plains, and vice versa. Even Greenwich and Old Greenwich look for individual distinctions rather than common ground. The climate and the scenery may be similar down the Mid-Atlantic, but the energetic people in their tightly packed enclaves find humanhood in knowing their place, identifying with it, and generally staying inside it for comfort and protection.

Californians know few such distinctions once within the borders of the nation-state. They were mostly mobile creatures in the first place, having come west in an act of daring or desperation. Once in the West, they tended to keep moving; Californians hold the national record for changing households, with families moving on the average of once every three years. Unlike an Eastern family that might shift from one side of Sheepshead Bay to another or—if it had a windfall—from Riverdale up to Westchester County, Californians in motion may cover huge swaths of territory. A move of one hundred fifty miles—from San Diego to San Fernando Valley, for instance—is not rare in Southern California. And it is not nearly so threatening to the movers themselves as is, say, a fifty-mile move in the East from Boston to Providence. From Boston to Providence means crossing state lines, means going from one entrenched culture to another, means worrying about whether one will be accepted by those heretofore strange people in the next city.

The moving Californian has no such worries. He or she can count on finding similar people in the new neighborhood, many of them hardly longer entrenched than the newest arrivals. The moving Californian has little cultural baggage to bring, and little cultural shock to anticipate. And since the Western family understands that it is a migrant unit among other migrants, it tends not to look for identity or stability in the cul-de-sac or the housing tract or even in the surrounding town.

For decades, there's been a folk mythology about Californians identifying themselves by where they came from rather than where they are: the annual Iowa picnic in Los Angeles, for instance; the English colony in Hollywood, for another instance; or the Southerners who spread themselves out along the San Bernardino Freeway. As in all mythology, there's a certain amount of truth in Iowa-picnic stories. Many varieties of Californians indeed refer to themselves by origin. Some of them are Iowans. But most of the rest are minorities: the Mexicans who moved north, the blacks who moved west, the Asians who moved east, and the elderly who've come from colder pieces of the United States to warm their declining years in California sunshine.

The state picnics are primarily elderly affairs. Retired citizens who come to California tend to use the West as a place to sleep and breathe, but not a place to earn livings, raise families, or discover personalities. It is perfectly logical for such people not to recognize California as anything but a depot, a final station to be enjoyed after the major chores of life are done. When they meet each other in Santa Monica as Chicagoans or Bostonians or Baltimoreans, their old-country loyalties are understandable and descriptive.

But younger Californians of working and child-begetting years tend to think of themselves as being without any background smaller than the state itself. Some exceptions survive in San Francisco, where city chauvinism is supposed to be another proof of sophistication. The majority of the others look for identification in what they do, not where they do it. An aerospace engineer, for example, may well have worked for Lockheed, Sunnyvale; General Atomics, La Jolla; TRW, El Segundo; and Aerojet General, Sacramento—all within one decade. He could have lived in all those towns while identifying mainly with his trade rather than his neighborhood. California technologists are modern Okies in many ways, forced to move where the work is and where the drought isn't. But they don't all come from Oklahoma or from one section of the country; they originally came from everywhere, and now they settle themselves wherever the contracts bloom.

Instead of seeking comfort and protection by identifying with a neighborhood, many Californians reject knowing their place or being labeled by it. "We don't belong here" takes on new meaning. The same lack of community pressure that permits children to avoid Sunday school and Little League if those institutions don't suit them is what allows Westerners within the same block to ignore the neighborhood and concentrate on more private matters of membership.

There are Westerners who, with pride abursting, announce that they were born here. "Here" invariably means California, not the particular city they now occupy. The native is something of a rarity in a state of refugees, and the native often feels—justly—that life along the ocean was more pacific before the other millions came to squat and settle. But the natives consider themselves citizens of a nation-state and not a neighborhood. With all California's internal differences of temperature and terrain, there is a kind of kinship that has successfully defied attempts to split the state in two, with a California of the North located above the Tehachapi Mountains and a California of the South dominated by Los Angeles and San Diego.

I think one of the reasons Californians refuse to pledge allegiance to community-sized pieces of real estate is our disenchantment with the small towns or small minds we once called home. California is full of refugees from Winesburg, Ohio, where the Midwestern, middle-class, middle-brow façades covered a mess of personal pathologies. California also has the creatures from the East who decided not to conform to the values of West Newton or East Greenwich. Depledging allegiance is a powerful force in the West. We don't belong here. The depledger can blame a place and not his or her own person for what once went wrong somewhere else. We don't admit personal blame here.

I've heard Californians brag, in an excess sense of classlessness, that there are no neighborhoods on the wrong side of the tracks in the West. With so few tracks anywhere, there could hardly be a wrong side or a right side.

That's not quite true. Freeways, for instance, serve some of the same snobbish purposes of social division. Even Watts, where the 1965 riots were, may be divided. A family living on the east side of the Harbor Freeway is in the midst of inadequate housing, grinding poverty, rampant unemployment, and high crime. A family on the west side of the Harbor Freeway is in a slightly fancier poor community, where there is a certain amount of economic stability and social mobility. The modest aspirations for mobility on the east side of the freeway are usually based on a move over to the west side.

The Santa Monica Mountains of Southern California also form a natural dividing line between human beings. Los Angeles is on both sides of the mountains, but there are marked differences in each basin. The southern section, usually called the L.A. basin, includes Bel-Air, Pacific Palisades, and the separate city of Beverly Hills. The northern section, usually labeled the San Fernando Valley, is mostly a basin of bedroom communities: Studio City, Sherman Oaks, and Encino. Encino is where upwardly mobile people live on their way to Beverly Hills. To move up the hill across Mulholland Drive into Beverly Hills or Bel-Air is to celebrate a change in status. "Oh, you live in the Valley" is and has been a way for Southern Californians to draw unkind distinctions.

So there is a small amount of geographic identification in the West, tagging people by putting them in their place. But the individual tags rarely stick. The bodies are too often in transit, even to and from Beverly Hills, which is a land-locked island completely surrounded by Los Angeles and its larger basin.

Putting people in their place does happen in San Francisco and the Bay Area to a larger degree. The Bay Area likes to consider itself older and wiser than upstarting Southern California. The Berkeley campus of the University of California calls itself Cal, for example, while the younger campuses are known as UCLA (University of California at Los Angeles) and Riverside

(University of California at Riverside). And the Cal students at Berkeley tend to look down on the citizens of lower California, feeling themselves cosmopolitan and feeling the others to be country cousins. There is an exquisite irony in such sophomoric elitism, because the bulk of Berkeley students are from Southern California in the first place, young people who've moved away from their parents to enjoy their own depledging privileges. You may remember the two students who wanted to live together for the rest of their lives until they each confessed to having come from Los Angeles.

But the Los Angeles child who becomes the Berkeley student and depledges allegiance to home is only following in Father's or Mother's footsteps. The Cal students are indeed consecutive generations of the nation-state, where home towns are for leaving and not for returning.

I once tried to identify the people of Los Angeles by topography rather than place. Los Angeles is too big to be a city, even in the New York or Chicago sense. Los Angeles covers more than four hundred sixty square miles, grounded in desert sand on one side and ocean sand on the other, a truly incredible stretch of the American imagination that defies sensible description. But within those political boundaries are all the old suburbs that were jokingly supposed to be in search of a city and all kinds of physical arrangements on which to settle. So I was examining the differences between people who wanted to live with water as opposed to those who chose mirages.

Several obvious categories came to mind: the beach people, the desert people, the mountain people, the canyon people, the valley people, the flatlanders. Beach people tend to want to know infinity is out there, as an escape. Desert residents find security in dry solitude. Mountain folks are most comfortable when they feel themselves above the human battle. Canyon settlers look for shelter and preserve some relationship to the womb. Valley dwellers like looking up from the bottom of the bed. And flatlanders enjoy the certainty of sidewalks and curbs in consistent grid patterns.

Los Angeles did seem more comprehensible when sliced in such physical terms. But I could carry topography only so far before I crossed other borders and the whole business blurred into areas, regions, and the entire state. The beach people, for instance, are similar in San Diego and San Francisco and Santa Barbara; the coast connects all of them and makes them more like one another up and down the state than they are like their immediate inland neighbors. If physical rather than political dimensions are used to define the settlements, then the whole state must once again become the basic carving board.

The East, especially the Boston–New York–Washington axis of Eastern power, does not have such astonishing variety of terrain. None of the great Eastern cities has the peculiar peninsular character of San Francisco, none has a mountain range in its midst as Los Angeles does. The beauty of the East is generally green and gentle; the beauty of the West is stark and burnt. Where the topography does not create its own distinctions, the human-made boundaries become more important. Manhattan Island does not look like an island, but its people have built their own separations from Queens, Brooklyn, and the Bronx.

I think Richard Farson, the behaviorist, is a living example of a Californian's freedom from place, of the way a Westerner moves about statewide space to go where the situation suits him at a particular moment in time.

Farson, along with Carl Rogers, started the Western Behavioral Sciences Institute in La Jolla, and together they were leading spirits in encounter grouping: Rogers, the elderly benign humanizer; Farson, the handsome young proselytizer. La Jolla was good soil for the groups. The citizens had means— enough time and money to want to deal with their problems. The San Diego campus of the University of California was just being built above the cliffs. Jonas Salk's spanking new research facility was moving in near the university. *Psychology Today* was just up the road at Del Mar. Farson was amidst other explorers. For a time in the late sixties he was president of WBSI, a mover of movements, concerned with womens' rights, childrens' rights, and educational change.

Then WBSI itself changed personality. Rogers and some of his followers began the Center for the Study of the Person, also in La Jolla. Some of the other Western Behavioral people stayed on to concentrate on more external matters of human relations. And Farson moved to Los Angeles to head the design school at the new California Institute of the Arts.

Cal Arts was a fresh challenge, an overnight institution endowed with Walt Disney money, blessed with a faculty of practicing celebrities, located on a knoll in the new town of Valencia. Farson would bring architects and planners and behaviorists together to create a multi-disciplinary approach to design that

216

would make human beings at one with humanmade forms. The idea of a behaviorist as boss of such a school was at once radical and appealing. Why not? Another mark of optimism.

It lasted a couple of years. Cal Arts had larger problems, including a board of trustees that didn't quite understand a faculty of performers, a faculty of stars who didn't want to teach so much as create, a student body of would-be artists whose romantic grasp exceed their technical reach. There were tensions between the board and the administration and the faculty and the students. Farson stayed long enough to learn some lessons in academic politics and then moved on again, to become the president of Esalen Institute, the pioneer human-potential experiment of Big Sur and the Bay Area. Esalen is where Farson is as of mid-1974, offering his considerable experience in human encounter from one end of California to the other. His book *Birthrights* is a manifesto for the children's movement which suggests, among other things, that children should have the perquisite to make choices in matters of where they live, with whom they live and under what circumstances. Farson's rights for children are rights already assumed by California adults who left home and parentage to make their way in the West. It all fits.

In the East, a man who moved as fast as Farson would be considered fickle, if not frivolous. In California, Farson can relocate whenever he wants to, taking his discipline and keeping his dignity each time he goes.

My own childhood happened in a portion of Westchester County, and the way my parents described where they lived is a basic lesson in the way New Yorkers know their place, or pretend to place. The family home was technically in Yonkers, then and now an industrial city. No one really wanted to live in Yonkers, because Yonkers wasn't pretty or green. And my parents had an excuse for claiming other turf as their own; there were nearer towns. There was Bronxville, for instance, which had big-name value and snob appeal. Once in a while I caught my father claiming a Bronxville home when he was far enough away from people who really knew the immediate neighborhood. There was Crestwood, in fact another part of Yonkers, but with suburban identity and a railroad station all its own. There was Tuckahoe, which was indeed the nearest village to the family home. Tuckahoe had a charming sound, but Tuckahoe was a relatively poor suburb housing the people who worked for the people in the fancier houses of surrounding towns. As a child I liked to say I came from Tuckahoe, because it sounded tough. My folks, depending on the company and the distance from home, always owned up to Westchester, but rarely admitted their Yonkers address. And they weren't snobbish people; they were Eastern people who understood that a person was immediately judged by his or her immediate neighborhood. And whenever I visit, the people in that neighborhood still confuse their own labels in Yonkers shame.

-XIV-

Stay Where You Are

One of the working titles of this book was *Only You Can Kill California*, addressed to the East Coast elders. But too many California books, by coincidence or symbol, already came as death notices: *How to Kill a Golden State*, *The Last Days of the Late, Great State of California*, *Anti-California*, and others.

But the working prejudice remains: The only way California can save itself is with outside cooperation, in the form of slowed in-migration, and with outside tolerance, in the manner of leaving us alone. The East has the power—money, media, political muscle—to make California another New York any time it wants to.

And talk about power—I once fantasized what the energy crisis could do to the West. I called the piece "In from the Cold," and worked myself into the following frenzy:

They still talk about the winter of '73-'74, how it changed the shape of America and made all master plans obsolete. It began with the energy crisis, which was a strange thing that everybody predicted but nobody prepared for, and they passed the blame around to big business and bad government and a bunch of Arabs.

What the energy crisis did was keep people at home, because they couldn't buy gasoline, and then it kept people cold at home, because they couldn't buy enough heating oil.

Nature didn't help.* Right around the New Year of 1974, Rochester, New York, suffered the worst blizzard of the decade. At the same time, Scranton, Pennsylvania was hit with a record cold snap. There were power blackouts and broken telephone lines as the ice came down to cover a city. Late January was worse for Groton, Connecticut, and Providence, Rhode Island. Lower New England was frozen in its tracks—its ill-serving railroad tracks—for two weeks. Buses broke down—when they had found gasoline in the first place. Several elderly people reported cases of frostbite caught in their own living rooms.

The rest of New England was iced over by early February. The hardy people of Maine, Vermont, and New Hampshire were confident at first; they were used to cruel winters, and they were historically skilled in tending their fires, their freedoms. But when sub-zero temperatures continued without a break for the whole month,

* Here is where my fantasy was disproved by the mild reality of that winter.

even the proud stoics of the Northeast started to panic. Livestock died. Schools closed. And Lem Garvey of Bangor, Maine, lit a new precedent by committing suicide in his home oven, curling up inside and then closing the door behind him. The oven was set at maximum baking heat. Garvey had made sure the gas was still working. Garvey also left a note for his neighbors before baking himself: "I'll be more comfortable going than staying," it said.

In Cornish, New Hampshire, 134 people died during the mid-February blizzard. They named the tragedy the New St. Valentine's Day Massacre. In New Bedford, Massachusetts, a madwoman calling herself "the spirit of Lizzie Borden" raided the morgue one night and chopped up several bodies, claiming she wanted to take them home for fuel. She was subdued by two deputy coroners and taken to the unheated jail.

The thaw did not come until April. By then, the survivors were weak, furious, and restless. They started moving away from the East Coast. They hoarded gasoline and packed up food and carried themselves to places where the cold couldn't kill them any more.

Nearly one million Easterners simply went down to Florida. More than two hundred thousand couldn't afford to go that far, and so they stopped to set up house in Georgia and South Carolina.

More than two million Americans from the East suddenly arrived between the Texas Gulf Coast and New Orleans.

And nearly five million made their way to

California. The San Bernardino Freeway was paralyzed for one week in May 1974. The Southern California Counties of Ventura, Los Angeles, and Orange could not accommodate the bodies once they broke through the freeway blockage. Not enough hotels, not to mention not enough hospitals, welfare agencies, restaurants, or even supermarkets.

The Los Angeles Department of Water and Power said it didn't have enough power to provide for the present population, much less the invasion. The Southern California Association of Governments sat in emergency session to set up airlifts for Wyoming. The California Chamber of Commerce hired 3,200 advertising copy writers to begin brochures that would make Montana more attractive to migrant Americans, omitting the mean temperatures from September to June. The governor's office in Sacramento applied to the White House for a grant equal to the annual state budgets of eight Eastern states. And movie producer Irwin Allen, creator of such disaster epics as *The Poseidon Advenutre,* started filming the influx for a mammoth documentary tentatively titled *West End.*

Silly as this nightmare now looks, California remains vulnerable to all kinds of conditions in the rest of America.

In the late sixties University of California geographer D. B. Luten was writing, "First, note that California cannot continue to grow forever, or even for a very long period, at a greater rate than the nation.

222

Simple arithmetic shows that if California maintains its growth rate at the traditional 3.8 per cent per year and the nation maintains its rate at the 1.6 per cent of 1960, then in about 110 years, say 2070, the population of both the United States and California would be about a billion. That is, all Americans would live in California. This seems unlikely."

Fortunately for Luten and the rest of us, the arithmetic changed, and so did the birth rate. But the geographer had a value judgment to offer back then that is valuable right now, even as the West has slowed its boom: "California will stop growing one day because it will have become just as repulsive as the rest of the country."

Luten contributed this dreary law in an article called "The Dynamics of Repulsion" for Carey McWilliams's book *The California Revolution.* He looked around the Golden State and found there were grounds for repulsion already in progress: polluted air, polluted water, poor urban transport, urban slums, unemployment, disturbed minds. The repulsive characteristics were, of course, the by-products of growth. But also, of course, there could be no solutions to those problems without new jobs. And new jobs mean growth. And growth means more repulsion. "On this merry-go-round," wrote Luten, "which is cart and which is horse?"

A peculiar and repulsive argument developed in California's Alameda County in 1973. One William T. Leonard, executive vice-president of a Bay Area builders' association, studied an action by the California Water Resources Control Board and concluded that Alameda couldn't qualify for federal antipollution funds any more, nor for state funds either, unless . . . unless thirty-one thousand people moved out of the county and stayed out until 1975.

Leonard appeared in *California Builder,* a trade publication, as an outraged, angry man. No government money for treatment plants. No funds for sewage purification. No allowances for Alameda without a population shrinkage.

What had happened was the drawing of a population curve to which Alameda had to conform. Below the curve were some furious conservationists who figured that limiting water was one way to stop growth. We'll soon deal with other Westerners who've looked for the proper formula for controlling the coast, but the Alameda anguish assumed *Alice-in-Wonderland* proportions under Leonard's leadership.

He proposed a lottery to select leavers, a kind of draft in reverse. And he insisted that all county officials be included in the drawing. The eviction of thirty-one thousand residents would vacate some seven thousand dwelling units, and any fool could figure what such overnight vacancies meant to the building trades, the real-estate business, and the lending agencies.

I speculated at the time: "Bay Area people are entrenched sorts. They tend to think they're wonderful just for being up there, just for being. Imagine how they might feel if the lottery not only pushed them out but told them where to go.

"Imagine them being ordered to Southern California; there'd be riots at the reduction centers and thousands of citizens would be trying to prove

224

physically unfit for duty in the smog theater. I figure the doctors and lawyers of Alameda County are already busy serving clients who anticipate possible appeals. No one has yet grappled with religious grounds as a reason for refusing to move, but I'm sure some sort of conscientious-objector status will be worked out for those too pious to battle life in Los Angeles."

Then I shifted to the notion of recruiting an all-volunteer army of Alameda defectors: "Surely if the financial inducements and flee benefits are made attractive enough, anyone can be seduced into moving anywhere."

The whole West once seemed repulsive to Americans. But the government wanted a railroad across its waistland, and so the Homestead Act, promising free land for venturesome settlers, became a motivating force.

My friend Edgardo Contini, planner and engineer and futurist, has advocated population dispersion for more than a decade, suggesting that America must offer inducements to shove bodies away from its two coasts. Contini's theories include a definition of an optimum city, roughly one million people in size. Smaller cities don't have enough numbers to insure culture, socio-economic-racial mix, and major educational facilities. Larger cities have so many numbers that culture and mix are destroyed by density. By Contini's standards, Boston and Seattle make much more sense than do New York and Los Angeles.

Los Angeles, however, has been slow to accept such ideas. During Sam Yorty's twelve years as mayor, Los Angeles kept a recruiter in New York. Even while we advocates of Lesser Los Angeles were screaming for a more modest megalop, Yorty had a high-salaried city servant on the opposite coast trying to lure large businesses to the West.

We proposed that the money could be better spent promoting Wyoming and Montana as magnificent alternatives for making new lives. Los Angeles, so rich in the resources of show biz, promotion, and advertising, could have employed creative talents for the making of brochures and films and slogans for population dispersal. I even thought we could have planted a few people in the chambers of commerce of Butte, Casper, Billings, Cheyenne, paid for by Californians to Diminish California.

Los Angeles, I later discovered, was already being used as a model of repulsion by its neighbor city, San Diego. During the local elections of 1973, San Diego candidates made Los Angeles the number-one issue.

"Nobody down there," I wrote, "wants to look like us up here. City Council aspirants view us with alarm, pointing a waggling warning finger north at Los Angeles and calling us a hideous mutation of growth gone mad."

A San Diegan told the California League of Conservation Voters, "We're the eighteenth biggest city in the country and anxious to become the nineteenth." That was a remarkable switch for the southernmost big town in California. Only three and a half years earlier, San Diego had been bragging loud about having grown up to become the second biggest city in the state. When San Diego passed San Francisco in population, then-mayor Frank Curran whipped off a wire to then-mayor Joseph Alioto, crowing about the change in rankings. And one of Alioto's deputies was silly enough to send back congratulations, saying something fatuous about being third and trying harder.

That was precisely when Lesser Los Angeles was born, and when other Californians said it was already too late, about one million bodies too late.

By the time San Diego council candidates were making L.A. an ugly issue, the western repulsive sprawl had already blurred the old boundaries between the cities. The tracts and the realty flags and the condominium complexes were unfurled all over the once-open territory. Orange County, between L.A. and S.D. was the fastest-growing region in Southern California. The old no man's land separating the two big cities was filled in; it was everybody's land, and leveled. It looked like the invaders had already won the war, and the politicians, as usual, were one campaign behind reality.

I've never quite given up on Los Angeles as a livable place, probably because a New York refugee doesn't make extravagant demands on a place of asylum. Compared to New York, Los Angeles has always seemed so much less dense and diseased. And not so long ago a New Yorker himself confirmed the relativistic approach to urban unhappiness. "Each year," the New Yorker said, "they tighten the valves a little more." He turned his hands in front of him and ground his teeth in a grotesque grimace. "So you've got a little smog out here," he continued, waving one hand as if to clear the air and dismiss it simultaneously. "I remember the first time I saw the West Coast. I was in the Army. About to go off and fight in the Pacific. Scared. Well, California was the perfect debarkation point for a man about to risk his ass for his country. Your roads were lousy. Your restaurants could kill. And your peasants—barbaric. If you could survive Los Angeles in the early forties, then you were probably basic-trained for the most dangerous place on earth. Now you have curbs. For a place where the automobile is so goddamn important, at least you've stopped the carnage. I can eat your food now without fear of dying from anything worse than mediocrity. And I find I can converse with the natives. It's all relative, this preposterous argument between East and West. Now that you're more like us, I might even consider life here."

That New Yorker is the kind of person who helped Easternize California. He may not enjoy the pathologic terror of the East, but he appreciates cities and high-rises and human compression.

Funny, his story of his first visit, hyperbole or not, is the reverse of the conventional wisdom on how California came to be what it is today. The westward-moving servicemen were supposed to be what brought the tidal waves of immigration after World War II. Unlike the basic-trained New Yorker, most young people on their way to the Pacific saw a peaceful shelter in the West, a place of sweet climate and serene pace. It was somewhere worth being mustered out to once the war was over. And once they were working their way through the Pacific, California looked even better. Non-combat days on such languid islands as Oahu and Midway and Guam accustomed them to life under strong sun; their circulatory systems slowed down, and their psyches depressurized to suit.

228

The California boom was a spoil of war. It happened in my case, too, although it was a smaller war. I was a military misfit during the Korean conflict. I had asked to be assigned intelligence chores, and I was ordered to radar duty instead. I had applied for service in the Atlantic, and was sent to the Pacific instead. I had wanted to be land-based, and was assigned to an aviation squadron instead. I was stupid. The U.S. Navy, against my wishes, had me in Hawaii for the better part of three and a half years. And suddenly a New York chauvinist was transformed into a Pacific beach bum. I'd never felt trade winds before, never known the pleasure of a house hanging off a hillside, never realized how many colors an ocean could contain until I was away from the gray of the Atlantic. When I left the service and went back to New York (mostly because the Navy would ship my belongings to point of enlistment, and I hadn't been able to find any work in Hawaii), I suddenly felt homeless and oppressed. Mainly oppressed.

I lived in the East for almost five years between the Hawaii hitch and the move to California. Each of those years was more difficult than military service.

I was a California convert from the moment I arrived in 1959. And all of us know that of all believers, converts are the worst kind. Too much fervor. An early act of fervor was the ungracious attempt to devise ways of keeping other refugees out of California. I took to writing about every evil under this sun, hoping my magazine stories might discourage migration to the West. I repeated all the horror tales about smog and freeways and kookiness, because I didn't want to see my old friends and neighbors and relatives following

229

in my fleeing footsteps. That was dishonest. It was also ineffective. Bodies kept coming through the sixties, undismayed. In-migration didn't diminish until the aerospace layoffs of the late sixties, the earthquake of the early seventies, and the intolerable inflation of the Nixon years. Just short of Luten's law on repulsion.

Television, some seers think, has almost as much to do with the California crowding as the Second World War. Once color came along in the sixties, the Rose Bowl game and Rose Parade made millions of malcontents between Maine and Maryland. Every New Year's Day thousands of Easterners decided to make their move. While they huddled around their television sets on January 1, there was snow and below-zero cold or bone-freezing wind—or all of the above—outside their houses. And on came the picture from Pasadena.

The sun was shining in Pasadena at the apogee of winter. Attractive people in shirt-sleeves lined the parade route. Attractive young women in less than shirt-sleeves posed atop the parade floats. Attractive cheerleaders wore shorts and no goosepimples during the big football game. Attractive spectators didn't even bring blankets. Suddenly the Eastern audience could see that somewhere has sunshine year-round, that some Americans tanned for more than two weeks a year.

The television picture from Pasadena aroused an orgy of discontent. The Rose Bowl has been one of the best recruiting devices ever presented under the guise of sports spectacle. Thank God the Rose Bowl also has an army of Eastern detractors who love to write about what's wrong with inane pageantry, who take perverse

pleasure in trying to convince people that there's
something wrong with being warm on New Year's Day
and something sinful about nailing flowers to a float.
The detractors, afraid of enjoying themselves, out of
season or in season, are a sort of national holding
action. Were it not for California's bad press, I'm
afraid maybe Luten's projection—all Americans living
in California by 2070—might have come true much
sooner.

In a spirit of fairness, the Americans who've always ground the sharpest axes against California have
generally come from the more intelligent classes. You
don't meet many unskilled laborers who develop reasons for despising warm weather or disliking fluid
sociology. If it is true that only intelligent people learn
to find fault with the West, then it may be hypothe-
sized that the West hasn't had its fair share of brains in
the long boom. Suppose there are three brilliant people, twenty-five quite bright people, forty-four average
people, and twenty-eight below-average brains among
every one hundred citizens. If such arbitrary arithmetic were assumed and if, out of every twenty-eight upper intelligences, there were twelve California detractors, then California would be attracting a smaller
proportionate number of good minds within the
westward movement.

Earlier, I tried to argue that only the most venturesome Americans uproot. Now I will allow that the
most venturesome may not necessarily be the most
intelligent. Uprooting is a small risk. And avoiding
risks often is a sign of superior thinking.

Let me add another theory on the demeaning of
the West. Perverse pleasure is a joy reserved for pre-

tentious minds. Any writer or social critic can deplore obvious poverty, rampant crime, and immobilizing snowstorms. There's no mental agility required in finding fault with life in the East. Ah, but to knock California, there's the fun. Only an exquisite sensibility, a refined and cultivated taste, can take on the Golden State of California and tarnish the living daylight out of it. I'm sure the English felt the same way about the colonies. After all, the English were the dominant people of Europe, the inventors of the Industrial Revolution, the makers of the Magna Carta. They were well educated and they were powerful and they lived in bleak soot-covered cities. The best way to justify life in drab weather in drab clothing in drab factory towns was to deplore life elsewhere. Only yahoos and undesirables would want to settle in a more comfortable surround.

I wish the detractors' holding action were more effective. I wish such organizations as Lesser Los Angeles were more than a wishful joke. I wish California did not have to rely on earthquake and unemployment to discourage Easterners from swapping coasts.

In the late sixties, an Australian historian, R. T. Appleyard, studied westward movement for Americans. He suggested that we may be such a mobile people that we won't stop at the California coast, we won't observe the Pacific as a natural limit, we will one day hardly hesitate to cross the ocean and set up new lives in the uncrowded continent of Australia.

California, in Appleyard's fascinating projection, would become a way station rather than a destination. He summed up statistics from Ray Allen Billington's

America's Frontier Heritage to buttress his case. Historian Billington, himself a California in-migrator from the Midwest, has described Californians as the most restless citizens of a restless nation. If one in every ten Eastern households is moved each year, one of every two and a half California households enjoys a shift each year. For every two passports issued on the East Coast, three Americans on the West Coast applied.

Appleyard discovered that America was sending increasing numbers of settlers to Australia, that most of them were from west of the Rockies. Americans went to Australia as cattle raisers and cotton growers. Paul Kahl, a 1961 refugee from Merced, California, told Appleyard, "We were under a continuing squeeze in California as to acreage and net income." Australia afforded him more of each, and he became extremely successful, along with his former partner in Merced, Frank Hadly.

During the late sixties, American interest in Australia increased some more. The Vietnam War was a factor, a disillusionment for liberals and a disaster of timidity for conservatives. While many young draft-evading Americans moved north, to Canada, many right-wing Americans moved west, to Australia. But even without the interminable agony of Vietnam, there were Americans who decided to exercise their restless rights by leaving their country, by leaving California. Some were sick of all the urban woes in the United States, the confrontations between races, between socio-economic groups; they wanted to go where there was room and time to avoid such unpleasantries. Some were sick of the roller-coaster

233

American economy, the ups and downs of aerospace and the stock market; they wanted to try a place that would keep growing. And some were the same kind of get-rich diggers who first went west for the Gold Rush; they wanted to unearth the next boom town, and so they moved Down Under.

Mobility is an American birthright, dammit, and that's one of the reasons it's so difficult to preserve the quality of life by trying to regulate the quantity of life on either coast.

There have been attempts in recent years to pass laws that would put lids on in-migration, serious attempts with ramifications much larger than the Alameda County diversionary tactics concerning anti-pollution funds.

The perils of Petaluma, for instance. Let us move on to the Constitution versus the Conservationists, in the next chapter.

-XV-

Keep the Rascals Out

Petaluma, California, was proud of its chickens; the people there used to brag about their little town as the poultry-raising capital of the world. A nice distinction, and not one likely to inspire challenge from more urban parts of the globe.

Petaluma's other handhold on fame came from the annual world wrist-wrestling championships, that timeless human exercise in which two people put their elbows on the table, lock grips, and apply opposing pressures.

Neither egg-dropping nor wrist-wrestling was among the more popular human obsessions in recent decades. Petaluma went its quiet way, a rural community about forty miles north of San Francisco, until the 1960s.

But two new pressures were applied to change

local life. Highway 101, the road between San Francisco and Santa Rosa to the north, became a freeway as it passed by Petaluma. And the suburban sprawl from San Francisco spilled up beyond Sausalito and San Raphael, over the Marin County line into Sonoma County and into once-pastoral Petaluma.

The population more than doubled in about one dozen years. There were fourteen thousand people living in Petaluma when the sixties began. By 1973, there were more than thirty thousand people, in addition to the hen houses.

Now, these newcomers were not Easterners, essentially; they were Californians who wanted to remain in the San Francisco area without living among the downtown sores of San Francisco. But they wouldn't have reached Petaluma if the whole West hadn't still been in the process of attracting Easterners and Southerners and Midwesterners.

The locals woke up with alarm at the turn of the seventies. It wasn't just the numbers that annoyed them; it was what the numbers had done to the town's life. Schools were on double session. The sewer system was becoming overloaded. Open lands were filling up with tract houses. The freeway had effectively cut Petaluma in two. On the west side of the road were the older homes, some of them graceful and gingerbready, others farmy, all of them familiar and individualized. On the east side of 101 were the subdivisions, stark and stucco, seeming to stretch to infinity, hammered up with a uniform lack of identity.

The old settlers were furious from the start. And the new settlers, once moved in with their mortgages, became furious. The old settlers didn't want to lose any more land to tracts; they wanted to keep the chicken flavor of the community. The new settlers didn't want to see any more people like themselves coming in to soak up overburdened services for which they were already overtaxed.

The city planning staff prepared a report for the Petaluma City Council, documenting what density had done to schools and sewers and open spaces. The council came up with abrupt controls in 1971; no new subdivisions for an entire year. Construction would be frozen in Petaluma until the planners and politicians could adopt comprehensive land-use policies and practices.

Housing was the hinge on which Petaluma tried to shut its doors, at least temporarily. If no new homes were available, no new residents could be accommodated—a radical approach to the population problem. Instead of hoping a growing mess would one day go away, Petaluma was trying to keep more mess from coming.

The people were pleased. They were also involved. In 1972, the citizens overwhelmingly approved a ballot initiative which would restrict future housing starts to five hundred residences a year. In 1973, the citizens endorsed that restriction by more than four to one.

Petaluma thought it had its problem licked for a while. City Manager Robert Meyer told reporter Phil Fradkin, "The opposition has not come out of the woodwork," a funny metaphor for construction controls. The city would select five hundred new houses on the basis of design, proximity to services, and desirable dispersal; a fifteen-member citizens' board would do the picking and keep all the development from happening in any one area in any one year.

By 1973, the opposition had come out of the woodwork, woodworkers all: The San Francisco, Peninsula, and Redwood Empire Home Builders brought suit. The Construction Industry Association of Sonoma County brought suit. They showed that some sixteen hundred housing units were rejected by Petaluma's preservationists during the year. They claimed that city governments do not have the right to deny landowners the use of their property, that city governments do not have the right to deny developers the opportunity to invest and profit, that city governments do not have the right to erase jobs in the building trades. The opposition was not without a powerful ally. The National Council of Home Builders plunked down twenty-five thousand dollars to help initiate the court battle. As the hinge swung in Petaluma, so might it swing across the United States.

Helen Putnam, mayor of Petaluma, felt the same way. She appealed to four hundred fifty California city councils and county boards of supervisors for help, asking for funds to sustain Petaluma's argument in the courts.

The results were not exactly a bonanza for Petaluma, but then, all cities everwhere plead poverty these days. By Thanksgiving of 1973, Mayor Putnam could thank twenty-five other cities and one board of supervisors for a total contribution of $6,965. But the results were also interesting because of where some of the money came from—San Jose, for instance. San Jose, like San Diego, used to brag about its boom. In the sixties, San Jose grew from a city of 200,000 to a megalop of 450,000, and the elected custodians of that explosion proudly claimed to preside over the fastest-growing city in California. But presumably San Jose has since learned a few lessons from such apparent prosperity. San Jose mayor Norman Mineta in 1973 wrote to Petaluma mayor Helen Putnam: "The city council of San Jose recognizes . . . the absolute requirement that cities be allowed the flexibility to meet the problems which result from uncontrolled, unregulated and rampant growth," and Mayor Mineta enclosed a check for $250.

The building industry's argument went to the Constitutional core, claiming the courts have traditionally upheld Americans' right of mobility and that the right to unrestricted travel includes the right to "abide and settle."

Petaluma's argument, in turn, was that a city has a right to regulate its own future.The builders tried to talk about the general welfare. The preservationists tried to talk about the specific issue of self-determination. Interesting case.

United States District Judge Lloyd Burke announced his decision in 1974. The Petaluma law, he said, was unconstitutional. "I'd prefer to live in a rural community," commented Burke, "but that doesn't allow the residents of a rural community to exclude others . . . what happened in Petaluma could happen in California, with the state setting a population limit and closing its borders."

Yes, exactly. Border closing has been a kind of California dream for some Westerners ever since the first New Yorker arrived with a troupe of actors, ever since the first migrant farmer decided the only way to beat the Oklahoma drought was by deserting Oklahoma. But such uncordial California dreams have always been properly labeled un-American and unconstitutional and undemocratic.

"The issue is relatively simple," said Burke, "It is the use of zoning by people who live there, versus those who want to live there." Well, maybe not quite that simple. After all, the people who sued were not necessarily people who wanted to live in Petaluma but, rather, businesspeople who wanted to profit from the people who might want to live in Petaluma. And the judge did emphasize that his ruling was not a mandate for Petaluma to "open its gates to unlimited growth." He told the city to evaluate future building applications "without regard to a policy intended to regulate population growth numerically," but that building decisions could be evaluated on "traditional zoning and community planning considerations."

This is where the Petaluma decision seems to become a kind of population paradox. A city may not decide people numbers but it may govern itself in matters of zoning and planning. If Burke left a loophole, it appears to be in language. Don't try to control human movement unless you dehumanize it —take it out of the house and call it an urban plan. Several California cities have since become confused.

Livermore and Pleasanton, both on the opposite side of San Francisco Bay from Petaluma, have passed citizen initiatives to regulate growth. Both Livermore and Pleasanton were quiet towns, good for grapes, until the suburban spill began to press at the vines with transplanted people. The neighboring winery towns used services as their hinge against wholly open doors; growth would be prohibited where municipal facilities did not exist to support new housing. A local superior court judge decided both Livermore and Pleasanton were too vague and ambiguous in their attempts to use facilities as a basis for controls. Pleasanton city manager William Edgar told reporter Daryl Lembke that both towns were in the process, in 1974, of preparing new local laws, less vague and ambiguous, that would specify the facilities necessary for supportable growth. They would use Ramapo, New York, as their example.

Ramapo, a suburb on the opposite shore, has enjoyed a rare success in the courts. Ramapo, too, used facilities as a basis for growth control. But Ramapo devised a point system to permit building, a positive approach to a desirable negative result. If a builder can show that a proposed development will be accompanied by adequate services and facilities, he or she earns points toward application approval. A federal court in New York found the point system constitutional because it is not based on Ramapo residents declaring Ramapo off limits to moving Americans.

Irvine, California, the scene of teen-age drug abuse described earlier, is trying to use the Ramapo approach in refining a planned community. Irvine city manager William Wollett told reporter John Gregory that the Petaluma precedent does not apply because no arbitrary numerical limits on growth have been set. "Under an emergency ordinance adopted last month," wrote Gregory in January 1974, "developers are issued building permits if they accumulate a certain mathematical score—'goodie points,' as they are nicknamed. Building applicants must prove that their

241

projects will not overburden existing or approved public facilities—water, sewer and drainage systems, police and fire protection, parks, roads, and mass transit corridors. Developers are given a certain number of points by city officials for meeting each public service criterion. If the entire building project is within five minutes' response time of an existing fire station, for instance, the builder wins five points. A score of 25 or higher qualifies for a building permit, provided that the project meets the normal municipal requirements."

The positive points approach begins to sound like a TV game show—*Schools or Consequences* or *Let's Make a Sewer*. But the battle to establish a legal basis for city self-determination versus American mobility continues, and may well determine the future of both coasts. In spring of 1974, Judge Lloyd Burke affirmed his earlier Petaluma ruling and issued a permanent injunction against Petaluma, forbidding the city from taking any action that would preserve, duplicate, reinstate, or further control by the numbers.

I've talked to a couple of California state legislators about what kind of law might be passed that would permit population control within the Constitution. State Senator Anthony Beilenson, himself an East Coast refugee, was not optimistic. He thought about the problem for a few weeks and said he'd rather not try to draft such legislation, although he could foresee some relief from growth pressures through the application of the facilities approach. State Senator George Moscone, Democratic floor leader and potential candidate for mayor of San Francisco, put his response on paper:

242

Certainly the subject commands the attention of 21 million Californians who take turns stepping on each other's toes. . . . On a national basis there have been considerable efforts in several state legislatures to provide an inadequate level of state and county assistance to welfare recipients on the ground that it would discourage in-migration and encourage an exodus of the poor to other states. I daresay we will never elect such an inhuman legislature.

There is, in my view, a legitimate and desirable way of restricting growth in California. Certainly no rational person can deny that much of California is poorly planned. Much of it is overbuilt and there is much more to be done in the creation and maintenance of open space, particularly in dense, urban areas. A statewide planning law directed toward the correction of these problems could not only be constitutionally enacted but would have the highly desirable effect of making life more comfortable for its inhabitants. Planned, rather than chaotic, development also has the pragmatic effect of discouraging the flight to California.

I trust I don't unduly insult your intelligence by pointing out that a measure of this kind would invite the wrath and considerable opposition of those who flourish under the name of "progress." There is no good reason, however, for the Building and Construction trades industries to join the opposition since any considerate legislator would include in such statewide planning scheme construction of rapid transit facilities, rural freeways, recreational facilities and the like.

Well, George Moscone is obviously trying to have his controls and his constituents, too—a perfectly reasonable posture for a politician. A statewide master plan would indeed help settle future densities by defining the denseness of future settlements. But I'm not optimistic about our ability to adopt a state plan in a state that resists government controls on everything —and the farther away the government, the more resistance aroused; the higher the level of government, the bigger the squawk. Before California adopts a master plan, more cities will have to prove to statewide doubters that master plans can work.

Once upon a simpler time I thought new towns might be the answer for California and other boom-bothered states—dispersal within the borders. But the so-called new towns built in the sixties in the West were mainly residential-commercial communities hiding behind the mask of a new term. They didn't have much age mix, much ethnic mix, much economic mix; when they were successful, they were homogeneous—primarily white, primarily middle class, primarily suburban subdivisions farther down the freeway. Private money, developers told me, could not expect a profit otherwise. Truly mixed new towns needed government subsidy.

A legislator who insisted on anonymity at the time said such subsidized new towns were not likely. Politicians respond to constituent pressures, and proposed new towns have no constituency until they exist. An elected official doesn't answer to an electorate that isn't there yet.

Only a federal decision to locate and build new cities would bring new towns into being. What all this

244

means is that neither East nor West can expect immediate relief from the nagging pressures applied to the sides of the country. Luten's repulsion is the reason why New York City is finally losing numbers, why Los Angeles may at last have stopped growing. Maybe we can keep them down on the farm if they've seen what downtowns have done to the country.

I read that California continues to grow, against almost everybody's better judgment. The state Finance Department's population unit said California added 203,000 bodies during 1974, for a grand new human total of 20.93 million. Only four counties, including Los Angeles and San Francisco, shrank. But even those figures are somewhat illusory in terms of megalopolitan densities. L.A. County still harbors 6.96 million residents, leading all the other fifty-seven counties of the state. And Orange County, just to L.A.'s southern flank, is the second most populous part of California, with 1.65 million. Making matters more congested, San Diego County, just below Orange, is the third most populous, with 1.5 million.

We were talking earlier about the development of the open lands between Los Angeles and San Diego, how one long strip of urbanity has been built along some hundred fifty miles of the West Coast. The Finance Department figures underline the swath of stucco; Orange County, between L.A. and San Diego physically, between L.A. and San Diego as most populous, is also the fastest-growing of the fifty-eight counties. Whatever small decline occurred in Los Angeles was more than made up for by neighboring Orange.

Maybe none of this bothers New Yorkers much;

after all, New York City, third largest in the world (behind Shanghai and Tokyo), has almost as many people pressed within its boroughs as L.A. and Orange Counties combined. And maybe Judge Burke is properly honoring our democracy when he insists that little Petaluma can't play numbers games against the Constitution. So let us deal with another kind of misery afflicting both coasts—and even the middle belly of America. It has to do with community character—and the interesting lack thereof. I like to call it "the french-fried franchising of the United States."

The last time I was in Petaluma, passing through during the summer of '74, I saw all the signs: McDonald's, Colonel Sanders' and A&W. The monstrous national chains of franchise foods have overwhelmed cities and suburbs and small towns. Travel writer Jerry Hulse described the phenomenon on a global basis several years ago. Hulse was taking a world tour, sponsored in part by a major hotel chain. After several days of jet-setting and bed-jumping, he woke up one morning with a minor headache and a major confusion. He called the front desk and said, "I know I'm in a Hilton, but what country is this?"

I know I'm in the United States of America when I pass an Arby's Roast Beef stand or a Baskin-Robbins ice cream parlor, but I have no idea what city it is. The domestic version of the Hilton dizziness is the Holiday Inn chain, with hundreds of look-alike buildings built all over the country. Holiday Inns are everywhere, beyond comprehension—is it possible that there are enough mobile Americans to fill most of those beds each evening? Especially when you realize that there are also Hiltons and Sheratons and Rodeways and

Ramadas and Best Westerns and and and and? Especially when you consider that some people must stay home? The Holiday Inn densities are themselves so extraordinary that I can count three of them within five miles of one another: There's the Holiday Inn Beverly Hills on Wilshire Boulevard and the Holiday Inn Westwood, also on Wilshire Boulevard, and the Holiday Inn Bel-Air. The Bel-Air version, a kind of concrete cylinder standing on end, is a reasonably perfect example of how a franchise flattens the character of a community by sticking up as a repetitive thumb. The concrete tube type of Holiday Inn exists all over California, thereby displaying the same quality in industrial Long Beach as in upper residential Bel-Air. Before the Holiday Inn came to Bel-Air, there were only two hotels in the area: the famous one named after the neighborhood itself, hidden under sycamore trees and protected by a swan moat, and a motel named the Sands, which was designed to hug the contours of surrounding hillside. Neither was offensive, or even particularly noticeable. But the Holiday cylinder is a can of commerce astride a fancy residential community, looked at but unloved.

There are sound economic reasons for the franchising of the States. Little stands by the side of the road can buy in big quantities because the parent franchise company supplies all its offspring. Hotels can offer sequential reservations to auto travelers from one central booking service. Travelers themselves can expect a level of consistency as they visit strange towns but stay with a hotel chain and eat in the franchises. Many millions of mobile Americans appreciate consistency over variety. For a restless people, we are remarkably unwilling to try something new. Like little children who will eat hot dogs every day but never taste liver pâté, Americans are addicted to the known, however bland or mediocre.

I blame us, not the franchises themselves, for the french-frying of the landscape. We are willing to buy chopped meat in cardboard boxes. We are willing to sleep under sparkly stucco ceilings. We are willing to sacrifice scenery for sameness.

Sameness is where the franchises spread into the central harangue of this book. The West should not be a curtain-walled copy of the East, any more than Manhattan Island should be the physical model for Manhattan Beach, California. I'm appalled that so many Californians have already swallowed franchises. But that seems to be the national trend, spurred by a tolerance for sameness, encouraged by mass-produced designs, fed by the success of franchises. "Bigness" is the one-word byword on both coasts.

I talked about California's unwillingness to be the window on the future earlier, about how it was the East Coast—specifically the East Coast media—that dumped the "test bed for tomorrow" mandate on people who are neither prepared for nor particularly interested in being a prototype for the rest of America. But even if Californians accepted such a role with pomp and glee, the country wouldn't conform to such expectations. Not when the money and influence and power live in Washington, D.C., and New York. The futures mandate is, at bottom, a sort of phony patronizing of the runaway children in the West, the same sort of smarmy phoniness you hear when an older generation tells its youngers that they will be the shapers and molders of tomorrow. In the very act of supposedly consigning the future, the elders are maintaining control of it, just as the philanthropist who endows a college keeps control of the kind of school it will be.

One of the reasons I'm glad California still resists playing Western Window is that it proves our disobedience to Eastern mom and dad. If we took the challenge, then they'd still be telling us what we should want to be when we grow up.

But I'm afraid neither the parental patronizing nor the spiteful disinclination are nearly as important as the reality of what's happening and what's being built and what's being merged in American life.

The franchises are but a symptom of the frenchfrying of urban character. Every major American city now has its ration of high-rising rectangles with geometric glass windows. Every American city has a downtown with depressed pockets of residential neighborhoods around its periphery. Every American city has overburdened its surface streets, overextended its capacity to protect and police, underplanned its highest function of offering community shelter to the broadest mix of humankind.

While I have my optimistic days, when the West still seems to have space and time left to build for the human dimension, the evidence suggests that California, too, is becoming a vertical labyrinth for packed rats who will begin to gnaw at one another as densitites increase while distance shrinks, who will not learn until after the repulsion level has been exceeded.

While I am not an enemy of technology, on nonoptimistic days I blame human ingenuity for making inhuman urban conditions appear possible. The Southern California climate, for instance, is an obvious casualty of the internal combustion engine, the freeway systems, the overwatering of the desert, and the sprawling of subdivisions. Smog is the most noxious and apparent by-product. But until the humans came in massive numbers with their combusting and their drenching, there was little need for air-conditioning in the West. California had shining days and cool nights until the crowds came. Now California is more humid than in its natural state. The back-yard pools brought water to the wealthy. They also brought water to the air.

Now the people of San Diego, like the people of Boston, live inside aritificial atmospheres in summertime. The indoor temperatures of Washington, D.C., are about the same as those of San Bernardino, California, although San Bernardino began urban life as a downtown beside a desert and Washington was lined with water.

Technology gave us the means of making uniform environments, a way of creating a whole new climate rather than coping with or controlling the original climate. It also gave us the illusion that we wouldn't have to pay exorbitant prices in terms of energy expenditures or outdoor effects of indoor regulation. Air conditioning is a supra-symptom of American sameness. McDonald's has it, as well as the quarter-pounder.

Heritage is supposed to be a bastion against loss of community character. Boston and Philadelphia do have corners of Colonial influence still facing the streets. Washington, D.C., still has its Paris plan with the wonderful radial streets that have strangers going in circles. But the East that exports heritage to the West is essentially New York, and the major heritage is essentially twentieth-century corporate, set and shaped in concrete.

California pretends to honor a Spanish past. We still have the chain of missions founded by Fathers Serra and Crespi as they worked their way up from Mexico, but those missions are mostly off the modern trails. What the new trails have are chains of Taco Bells, in which the word is "commerce" and the Spanish character is flat as a tortilla.

The Spanish influences in California almost always appear as part of a sales pitch, whether to sell tacos under tile roofs or to sell tract houses under romantic street names. I have a street map in front of me for a Los Angeles subdivision called, un-Hispanically enough, Laurelwood. It contains the following residential roads: Dona Pegita Drive, Dona Dolores Place, Dona Maria Drive, Dona Conchita Place, and almost two dozen other Donas of uniformly Spanish naming. The houses that line these lanes, however, are the usual Southern California composte of eclectisism: a Colonial column here, a modern cantilever there, a French mansard over there, an occasional suggestion of adobe down the block that turns out to be stucco painted in dung color.

California is about as Spanish as New York City is Dutch; there are a couple of labels left lying around, but the basic material is much newer, and any hints of heritage are from synthetic fabrics. Santa Barbara, a city with strict architectural controls, is one exception. Santa Barbara does have a certain Spanish style, with inner courtyards and curved doorways and red tiles on the tops of houses. But Santa Barbara, with its restrictions against industry and density, is no more typical of California than Williamsburg is representative of Virginia; they are both deliberate small samples of what was, not what is or will be.

I opened the downtown Los Angeles phone book for a suggestion of literal New York influences. Labels, again, but indicative of California's willingness to list the best sirloins on menus as New York steaks— homage to the old place, put to pasture. We have more than thirty-seven New York entries on the Pacific Telephone Company rolls, only a few of them branches off the home tree, such as *The New York Times* and the New York Life Insurance Company. Most of the New Yorks in Los Angeles are tributes to the mother country. New York Appetizing Store, for instance, is in the Fairfax area of L.A., where refugees from the Bronx have set up a series of delicatessens that might honor Fordham Road. New York Discount Store is homage to the idea that things cost less in the nation's biggest shopping center. New York Feather Company of California is a marvelous blend of both worlds; research time did not allow a visit to California's New York Feather Company, but the garment industry in L.A. is second only to Seventh Avenue. The New York Hair Conspiracy also trades on fashion's home base. The New York Hotel, oddly enough, is in the midst of L.A.'s Little Tokyo, a real landmark of East-West respects. And the New York Junk Company suggests only an expatriate salvage dealer who came west for salvation.

Now that Richard Nixon has come home to San

Clemente, less predictably than the swallows return to nearby Capistrano, many East Coast friends suggest that he was a uniquely California product: Yorba Linda boy made good at Whittier College, bundled in Navy braid for World War II, sent to Congress from his home state, raised to the vice-presidency because he came from the newly populous West, and finally upped to President, whence he eventually slid back like mud from an unstable house in the Hollywood Hills.

Unfair. Unfair to Nixon. Unfair to California. Such Eastern summaries fail to account for the Eastern contributions to what might have remained a California career. Californians, for instance, were not the forces behind Nixon's nomination as Eisenhower's running mate in 1952. East Coast party sages thought he would add to the ticket, while most Californians would have preferred Earl Warren, their less partisan, more experienced favorite son. Adlai Stevenson, Ike's opponent in 1952, tried to put a placemark on the rival ticket: "Nixonland," he said before Disneyland was invented, "is a land of slander and scare, of sly innuendo, of a poison pen and the anonymous telephone call, and hustling, pushing and shoving—the land of smash and grab and anything to win." Californialand, with all its vulgarity, is a place of happy vulgarity. Even if Nixonland existed in less hysterical terms, California is no such country.

And California, I would remind Nixonphobes, was where the former President lost his most inglorious election. The year was 1962, only two years after Richard Nixon came within a couple of whiskers—a couple of nationally televised debate whiskers—of first

253

winning the Presidency against John Kennedy. The race was for governor of California, a modest step down from living within a heartbeat of the White House. Nixon was running against Edmund G. Brown, an affable liberal who happened to be in some trouble with liberals because of the way he botched the execution of Caryl Chessman in 1960.

First Pat Brown had infuriated the believers in capital punishment by giving Chessman—then the longest resident of Death Row—a reprieve on most peculiar grounds of international diplomacy, because Dwight Eisenhower was in the process of visiting Latin America and author-convict Chessman had many emotional champions in Latin America. Then Pat Brown infuriated the opponents of capital punishment by executing Chessman after all, once President Eisenhower was safely back in Washington. The Brown-Nixon race was not memorable in the running. But it was unforgettable the morning after Nixon lost.

That was when the supposedly calculating and cold candidate told a press conference, "You won't have Nixon to kick around any more." He also promised in 1962 that he had just completed his last press conference.

He was wrong on both predictions. But it was California where Nixon received the most humiliating defeat of his political life. And it was in the East where Richard Nixon revived to eventually claim the Presidency. What Nixon did after blaming the California press for his licking was move to New York. New York was his base, as an attorney in a firm including John Mitchell, for the reconstruction of Richard Nixon. He became wealthy as a specialist in international corporations. And he became politically respectable as a tireless spokesman for Republicans, running all over the country. Richard Nixon did pay his party dues, over and over again, on every husting west of the Hudson. But it was New York, where Mitchell the one-time king-maker lived and where the corporate board chairmen lived, that helped Nixon claim fresh candidacy.

Even now, his closest friends are probably the East Coast friends: Rebozo of Key Biscayne and Abplanalp of New York.

Ronald Reagan, whom I grudingly admired earlier, is the uniquely California candidate. Born in the Midwest, he achieved minor success at a minor college and moved to California for eventual work in the movies as a cowboy and cardboard hero, while switching political allegiances from moderate Democrat to consummate conservative, becoming as tireless an after-dinner speaker at Republican causes as Richard Nixon but beating the same Pat Brown for governor in 1966, because he managed to assume a public common touch while never catering to the common man. Ronald Reagan, regardless of his policies, is not a local joke. He is a California creature, which is to say a refugee with a clear idea of where he's been and where his optimism can take him. But even such optimism is clouded by the french-fried franchising of the United States, by the theories of Luten, by the decision of Burke, by the difficulties of trying to save what's good without becoming fascistic about it.

If I were king—which is about as likely as my

becoming governor—I think I'd offer credits to people willing to disperse. Say, income-tax benefits to those Americans hardy enough to settle the colder states up North. Or low-interest loans to those willing to build in the empty middle. Or the promise of irrigation for newcomers in Nevada and Utah.

If barricades are un-American, blandishments are not. I'd give blandishments, much the way the United States seduced settlers with the Homestead Act. But now I'd use blandishments to make other places seem more attractive than California, if not in warmth and topography, then more attractive in more tangible terms such as food, land, and shelter. And yes, if I were king of the whole caboodle, I'd build new towns and cajole constituencies for them.

I don't want repulsion to be the reason for population control. When the kids were crashing out of California, I thought they were premature about damning their universe, because urban troubles are truly universal. But I could accept their desires to get away from home, just as we older Californians wanted freedom through fleeing. Now I notice the beginnings of a countermovement, however. Some young people are returning to California, having discovered the pain and plastic elsewhere. Some young people are even coming back to live in Southern California, a fate they once considered worse than purgatory.

Sure, I'd create a state plan such as Moscone suggests. But if I were king, I'd create a national population plan and use blandishments as the barter to assure compliance.

No blandishment would make me come home to New York. I see too much misery on my occasional visits. The people in service positions are still surly. The people in high-rise apartments are still frightened. The cab drivers are still angry at everybody who isn't one of them—and they insist on telling everybody who isn't one of them about it. But if my kingly proposals were adopted, even New York might thin out and be habitable again. And then we could all live happily, spread out, ever after.

-XVI-

Just Keep Moving

I began by saying that the first time I was ever attacked by a stranger was in Portland, Oregon. It was a dark and rainy night, as all horror stories should begin. I was driving back to my hotel room from a Reed College seminar on media and politics. I had been drinking after the seminar at the home of Reed President Paul Bragdon, himself a Maine-born, New York-experienced expatriate. The Bragdons insisted I borrow their car for the ride to the hotel—why take a cab at two in the morning, why not just bring the car back tomorrow and we'll take you to the airport in it?

Well, I did what any almost sane person would do who was driving in a strange car in a semi-strange town at a godawful hour in a sobering condition. I drove slowly.

On a residential street with cars parked along the

curb, I saw two bright white lights in my rearview mirror that rapidly were growing larger. I could not pull over until there was a hole in the curbside parking. That must have been a wait of about thirty seconds as I proceeded on my slow but sure way.When I did pull over to let the bright lights pass, the driver of the other car—a white Volkswagen—passed me at about forty m.p.h. with a long blare of horn. I said something scatological about him to myself and proceeded.

About thirty more seconds later, I turned left off the residential street onto a major highway and almost immediately pulled up to a red light. Next to me, in the adjoining lane at my left, was none other than the honking VW speed merchant. He turned to his right and offered the classic middle-finger salute. I may have smiled; I'm not sure. He seemed then to be shouting at me through his closed car as the light changed to green.

I pulled forward on the green, ignoring his gesticulating and apparent shouting. He roared forward and pulled his car athwart my lane, blocking my way. I stopped. And in that second or two of stopping, I checked to be sure my windows were closed and my doors locked.

He leaped out of his car, the motor still running. In the next second, I checked to see that he carried no visible weapon, that he was a young man in his midtwenties, that we were indeed on a wide boulevard. I probably could have backed up in the next second, lurched to my left around him and his car, and tried to make my getaway. I didn't. Maybe that was the first midjudgment by an urban man with long living experience on both coasts. But the idea of possibly starting a movie-style car chase in a semi-strange town in a strange auto at a godawful hour in a sobering condition seemed dumber than sitting still and hoping the incident would go away. The idea of both of us colliding, the idea of banging up a Bragdon car, was unappealing enough to keep me in my place. I even remember remembering that I wasn't carrying much cash, and so I wasn't much of a robbery prospect.

The angry young man came up to the driver's side and started screaming through the window. I couldn't quite hear his message, just feel his fury. I resolved to keep the window closed and hope a policeman or anybody would come along to interrupt our idiotic situation.

But then the young man started yanking at the door. And then he started wrenching at it, kicking the car body with his feet. My second possible misjudgment was to roll the window down so that he would stop damaging the borrowed car. After all, I thought in that second, I'm a person of reason, I'm persuasive, I'm innocent of doing him any more damage than slowing his speeding. We can talk. Well, he could talk. He could also hit. As soon as the window came down, his fist came in, with a smart hard jab to my chin. I was staggered. I hadn't even said anything yet. But my immediate impulse was to guard the door lock, meaning I leaned back toward the door, and his jab met me again. I must have looked like a child's bop bag, bouncing back to guard the door, being punched back toward the center of the car.

I tried to say something on my way up, and realized he was screaming as he hit. "You drive like a fucking white man," I heard. That was funny, even at that unfunny time. He was as white as I.

He grabbed the front of my shirt, the better to aim his jabs. I was busy guarding the door lock, trying to wrest free of his shirthold, and hoping somebody would pull up on the highway. I considered getting out of the car and trying to fight back. That seemed the dumbest option yet. He was younger, probably stronger, and certainly more experienced at this sort of meeting than I. And the car was giving me some protection; he could hit only the left side of my face.

I don't know how long the absurdity went on; it seemed like minutes, but may have only been fifty seconds of jabbing, "fucking white man" yelling, and growing fear. At first, even while making questionable decisions, I had a detached feeling about the fight. Some nut was out there hitting me without proper provocation. I was taking the hits, wondering whether there wasn't something else I should be doing at the moment.

I did make a reporter's mental notes on his physical characteristics: about 5' 10", brown hair, bushy mustache—almost Hemingway mustache, but no beard—long sideburns, brown leather jacket, dirty white T-shirt, uneven top front teeth. Not ugly. But mean. I never could figure out the disproportion of his outrage. Amphetamines? Insanity? He absolutely wasn't on any kind of downer—dope or alcohol—because he punched too precisely.

I was continuing to take notes and feel terror when suddenly, without a cue, he stopped and ran to his car. I remember thinking that maybe he knew he couldn't afford the waste of gasoline. But he never made any attempt to rob me. He jumped in, swung the VW to face the road, and roared off in a cloud of white vapor mixed with drizzle that prevented me from reading the license plate. While he had been pummeling, I couldn't read the plate because the car was broadside to me; now I couldn't read it because of Portland's wet winters.

I drove back toward the hotel, taking inventory of my wounds. Nose bleeding, but not hurting. Cheek bleeding and hurting. Buttons torn off shirt. Some blood drying on buckskin jacket. Eyes, hands, and feet working fine. Feet now starting to shake a little, nervous post-reaction. When I pulled into the hotel garage, a young attendant started toward the car, saw this bloody mess beginning to emerge, and turned to run away from me. "No," I shouted at him. "I'm a victim, not a robber. I got hit." He took the car, looking wary. Sweet modern irony. Attackees frighten people.

The next morning I looked worse. The blood was washed off, but my cheek, upper lip, and jaw were swelling blue. The whole left side of my face seemed to have been inflated and painted in abstract splashes of red and purple. When I returned the car, the Bragdons were horrified. Portland is no place for such violence. I agreed with them. David Bragdon, teen-age son of Nancy and Paul, insisted that I call the police. But I didn't have the license number, I said, and I wasn't more than surface wounded. I wasn't a robbery victim; he never even tried. But somebody else might have been killed by the same lunatic last night, David said, and I owed it to other victims, past or potential. I called the police. They allowed that there wasn't much they could do, even with my physical descriptions.

One of the reasons I tell this story here is the response I received when I wrote about it back in Los

Angeles. The return mail came in four major categories, in this order of weight: law-abiding people who said I was stupid; law-abiding people who were simply sympathetic; law-abiding people who said I deserved to be beaten if I had been drinking at all before driving; law-skirting people who told me what they do to avoid such things.

Most of the people who said I was stupid would have opted for flight in my situation. Flight failing, they would never open their windows under those circumstances, and I think I agree with them after the punchout in Portland. The sympathetic people wrote about the insanities of our times, how none of us are safe, how there's no predicting what may happen where, how there are no real remedies that make sense. The drink-hating people showed little temperance; they assumed I had been drunk—not true—and they seem to think drunks are fair game for muggers, robbers, and other thugs. The law-skirters—about one in every ten letters—scared me most. They wrote about the concealed guns they keep in their cars to brandish against any potential attacker. One man even claimed, anonymously, to have killed a young hood one night near Bakersfield because the hood had forced him to the side of the road and come toward his car much like the VW jabber had come toward me. Some wrote about the baseball bats, tire irons, and hammers they have used—not just brandished, *used*—as preventive weapons.

The mail didn't reassure me at all, because I suddenly had some idea of the numbers of Southern California neighbors who must drive around as mobile armories. East Coast people, I knew—or think I

263

knew—drove themselves to peculiar forms of personal protection. But I really didn't know there was so much paranoia—or well-placed fear, you may argue—in California.

Well, I've walked New York late at night in recent years. I even tried Central Park once, when journalistic curiosity overcame common sense. And nothing has ever happened to me. I've lived in Boston, lived in Philadelphia, made many visits to Washington, D.C., and spent twenty-three of my first twenty-nine years as a native New Yorker, always willing to be out and walking at night rather than in and worrying. And nothing ever happened to me. I've lived in California for fifteen years, always walking at night. And nothing ever happened to me.

Portland, a city of fewer than half a million bodies in a state of only two million bodies, was where senseless violence first hit me. Not while walking at all.

The immoral of the story, I'm sure, is that where you happen to be in this life is much less important than what happens to you once you are there. And so this entire East-West exercise should have made more allowances for exceptions, for luck—good and bad—for differences of the state of life within the state of California, for differences between the reticence of New England and the rashness of New York, for the undeniable fact that people shape places even as places shape people.

But generalizations seem to tumble into something sensible if you don't make allowances or build parentheses or hedge with "howevers."

The discontented teen-agers and the Luten theory of repulsion and the Western air of optimism and the

Portland punchout have some common grounds if we begin and end this exercise in terms of why people settle anywhere.

The prolonged adolescence of California, pimples and all, was based on feelings of opportunity, mobility, freedom, privacy, and pleasure. A person could be what a person wanted to be. A person didn't have to be defined by family name, home town, religious persuasion, or job. Job didn't govern joy, as it does in older societies. A Californian could go about his or her pleasure even as that Californian went about business; no one had to wait for a vacation once every summer to see the sunshine.

The California teen-agers who grew up repulsed and ready to run are the sons and daughters of adults who once did some running of their own. They are the logical descendants of adults who didn't want to be what their parents wanted them to be, who refused to have planned neighborhoods planned for them. Teen-agers who reacted to my Portland beating almost uniformly said I was stupid and then said there's always safety in running.

I've come to think that it isn't California that repulses young people but the prospect of having to settle down on someone else's terms.

California began with frontier feelings, but once it became the place of manifest density the frontier was crowded out of consciousness. Some of the frontierless frustrations of young people come from an understanding that there are no new places left—to go, to discover, to hide.

And now, in the mid-seventies, Americans are afraid of a new depression. Afraid of inflation, unemployment, loss of influence and lack of power. Americans everywhere are suffering from energy shortages—real and metaphorical.

So along comes a new kind of uniquely American optimist, the one who says a depression will be good for what ails us. These optimists include the offshoots of Reich's *Greening of America,* the fostered children of the hippie movement who still want to plant potatoes by hand. They include the communal thinkers who've been waiting for capitalism to die for decades now. They include the futurists, such as friend Toffler, who've been predicting a society based on swapped social services instead of manufactured goods. They include magazine writers such as Jesse Kornbluth, who suggests that a depression will only be a temporary, although painful, transition to a new lifestyle in which the environmentalism of *The Whole Earth Catalog* will finally come to life. And they include the likes of Peter Goldmark, once a technologist and now a social theorist.

Dr. Goldmark's first revolutions turned thirty-three times per minute; he invented the long-playing phonograph record. He was also big in the birth of color television, thereby bringing some added life to the McLuhan notion of a global village.

Goldmark has turned to the reinvention of rural America these days, insisting that Middle America does matter—or should—if we are to save ourselves from the mess of megalop at both sides of the country. He talks about the thirty million people who've moved to the major cities in the last thirty-five years, the most massive shifts away from the land in human history. He talks about the 90 percent of us who occupy only 10 percent of the American soil, the 10 percent below the high-rise curtain walls. He talks about how the crowding will be worse by the end of the century, how two out of three Americans will cram into one of twelve megalops by the year 2000 unless something sensible is done to reverse present directions.

Writer Kornbluth, in *New Times* magazine, predicted that Goldmark's back-to-earth answers might be just what the depression doctors ordered. We could return to rural life without becoming mere bumpkins because we could take cable TV and computers and copying machines with us. Goldmark would have one hundred million Americans resettle on six thousand uncrowded parts of the country, and his figures indicate that such a dispersion would only increase the growth of each area by only two percent.

A depression might accomplish what the people of Petaluma, in their unhappy new prosperity, could not: the redistribution of American bodies. A depression might be more effective than the blandishments I was about to offer, as king, in the previous chapter.

The prospect of depression does not lighten my spirit at all. Recommending it as the dosage for what ails us is uncomfortably akin to the radical thinking of the sixties that said repression had to be much more repressive before freedom could make a comeback. Any American at either end of the country has to hope we can proceed from where we are, without having to fall into the abyss before coming up again.

But maybe the character of California optimism is carryable. Maybe the quality of life that created the West is something that has to remain rootless if it is to persist. Maybe the way for all of us to find a life of quality is to keep moving—moving with a Western sense of reality that admits that too many people can be too much of a good thing, that understands children will insist on finding their own way, that includes the human capacity for pleasure as a necessary piece of baggage.

I think the great lesson we've learned in California is the danger of being locked in and the promise of staying in motion. In California, the going itself is good.